WILD FAITH

Believing God for All Things, and Living Like It

By Joel Wingo
Founder of 31 Feet Forward

Copyright, Acknowledgments, and Legal Notices

ISBN:
Hardcover: 979-8-9955046-3-4
eBook: 979-8-9955046-1-0
Paperback: 979-8-9955046-0-3

Acknowledgments

Special thanks to the many students, clients, friends, and ministry partners who have inspired the stories and lessons in these pages. Your faith and courage have helped shape this message.

Gratitude to the leadership and mentors throughout my life for modeling faith in action.

To the team at Share the Struggle Coaching, you make wild faith possible every day. Thank you for charging forward, 31 feet at a time.

Permissions and Attributions

Select quotes, lyrics, and stories are used by permission or under fair use guidelines for illustrative and educational purposes. These include:

Music and Lyrics

- **The Smashing Pumpkins.** "Bullet with Butterfly Wings." *Mellon Collie and the Infinite Sadness*, Virgin Records, 1995.

Movies and Films

- *Chariots of Fire. Directed by Hugh Hudson, Warner Bros., 1981.*
- *The Fellowship of the Ring. Directed by Peter Jackson, performances by Elijah Wood and Ian Holm, New Line Cinema, 2001. Quote originally from J.R.R. Tolkien's The Fellowship of the Ring (1954).*
- *Like Arrows. Directed by Alex Kendrick and the Family Life Films team, Family Life Films, 2018.*
- *The Matrix. Directed by Lilly and Lana Wachowski, Warner Bros., 1999.*

DEDICATION

For Everyone who has ever dared to believe God for more, even when it looked impossible.

To my wife, **Richelle**, your sacrifice and presence have marked every step of this journey. Through every high and low, you have remained by my side, even when it was not easy. What we have walked through together carries more weight than words can hold. I am grateful for the road we have walked. I do not know exactly what lies ahead, but I am grateful to have you beside me as we find out.

To my children, **Ava, Emma, and Eli**, you three have shown me the heart of a father and brought immeasurable joy into your mom and my life. You are the center of our world and the inspiration behind so much of our love, faith, and purpose. Our desire is for you to live this life with reckless abandonment for Jesus.

To my parents, **Bob, and Betty Wingo**, thank you for raising me in a God honoring home and for the unwavering example of faith you lived out together. Dad, your life shaped my vision for what it truly means to serve others. Mom, your constant support and quiet strength made every step possible. Thank you both for the countless miles traveled, the sacrifices made, and the time you gave so freely. Thank you for showing up to every sporting event and every season of my life. Your encouragement, faith, and investment in me are what true legacy is all about.

To my best friend, and brother, **Bobby Wingo**, thank you for always being there for me, patiently listening to my ideas and believing in what God could do through my life from the very beginning. Your steady presence has been a gift I deeply treasure.

To my sister, **Vicky**, thank you for caring so deeply and for always knowing the right words to speak when I need them most. Your kindness and wisdom have been a steady comfort and encouragement along the way.

TABLE OF CONTENTS

INTRODUCTION

THE JOURNEY TO WILD FAITH

I believed in God but built my life in a way that did not require much faith. For years, I followed Jesus and lived a life that looked faithful on the outside. Yet my prayers were careful and my dreams were small enough to manage. I wanted a faith that fit neatly into my life, one I could explain, control, and contain. I was sincere, but I was safe.

I grew up as a preacher's kid in a home where faith was everywhere. Scripture, worship, and ministry shaped the rhythm of daily life. Faith was not something we visited on Sundays, it was woven into family dinners, late night conversations, laughter, sacrifice, and seasons of struggle. I watched my parents walk through joy and heartbreak with quiet faithfulness as my father served as a minister. Their example gave me a strong foundation, but I eventually learned that a foundation alone cannot carry you through the moments when faith is tested. That foundation carried me for a long time. Until life asked more of my faith than a foundation alone could give.

Early in my college years, safe faith stopped working. The beliefs I had grown up with were true, but they had not yet been tested by disappointment, loss, or unmet expectations. I encountered moments when prayers went unanswered, plans unraveled, and dreams quietly faded before they ever had a chance to take shape. The faith I knew how to practice could explain Scripture, but it had not yet learned how to sit with doubt, unanswered prayers, or disappointment.

It was there, in that tension, that I found myself standing at a crossroads. Not between belief and unbelief, but between control and trust. Between a faith I could manage and a life that required daily dependence on Jesus. I had to decide whether I would continue building a life that God could bless from a distance, or whether I would risk following Him into places I could not manage or predict. I did not yet understand what it truly meant to lean on Jesus, and if I am honest, I still wrestle with that surrender today. But something began to settle deep in my heart. God was faithful, even when the path forward was unclear.

Even now, leaning fully on Jesus does not come naturally to me. My instinct is still to plan, to brace, to manage outcomes before I trust Him with them. I still wrestle with surrender. But over time, my heart and mind have been anchored in a deeper truth. God is faithful. Not occasionally. Not conditionally. Faithful in every season, including the ones I do not understand. It was in those uncertain moments that Jesus met me most clearly. Not by removing the tension, but by inviting me to trust Him within it. He did not give me all the answers I wanted. Instead, He offered Himself. I began to realize that faith was not simply believing the right things about God, but trusting a living Savior who was still speaking, still leading, and still calling me forward.

Slowly, my faith began to shift. I started praying prayers that felt bigger than my ability to control the outcome. I took steps of obedience without waiting for full clarity. I learned that Jesus does not only call us to believe in Him. He calls us to follow Him. To move. To live in ways that cannot be explained apart from His faithfulness. Faith stopped being something I possessed and became something I practiced.

I have watched God move in ways I could never have planned. I have seen relationships restored, doors opened, provision appear at the right moment, and purpose rise out of places I once only saw pain. Over the years, I have also had the privilege of walking with people as a life coach, ordinary men and women from different backgrounds and seasons of life People just like you. This book was written for anyone who senses there is more. More than routine faith. More than manageable belief. More than a life that never truly requires trust.

There came a moment when a single image gave language to what God was already doing in my heart. I encountered the story of the rhinoceros. A powerful animal capable of incredible momentum, yet with a surprising limitation. A rhino can only see about thirty feet ahead. Beyond that, everything is unknown. And yet, despite limited vision, it charges forward with full strength and confidence. That image stopped me. Because it mirrored the way God has always invited His people to move forward, step by step, trusting Him beyond what they can see.

I realized that much of faith is lived at the edge of vision. Real faith often begins at the thirty first foot. The place just beyond what we can see, plan, or control. Wild faith is not about having all the answers before you move. It is about trusting that God is already present in what you cannot yet see.

This book is an invitation to trust God with that next step. To move forward when certainty ends. To follow Jesus beyond comfort. To discover that obedience often unlocks purpose you could never reach by staying safe. If you have ever believed in God but quietly built your life in a way that did not require much faith, this journey is for you. The adventure of wild faith begins exactly where your vision ends.

An Invitation to the Adventure

If you are holding this book, I believe you are ready for something more. Not more information, but more trust. Not more certainty, but deeper obedience. Maybe you are standing at your own thirty first foot, staring into uncertainty and wondering if God can really be trusted there. My invitation is simple. Do not settle for safe faith. Step forward. The adventure of wild faith begins exactly where your vision ends.

Do not allow fear or hesitation to keep you from the fullness of what God has prepared. Step into the adventure one faith filled step at a time. Whether you feel confident or uncertain, strong or hesitant, this journey is not reserved for the fearless. It is for the willing.

Throughout these pages, you will encounter stories, Scripture, practical tools, and honest encouragement for the road ahead. My prayer is that you will see yourself in these words, and that you will find the courage to move, to trust, and to live with the wild faith God intended for you. So, take a breath. The journey begins now. Let us discover together what happens when we trust God with the thirty first foot and beyond.

Your friend in the journey, Joel

Chapter 1:
Welcome to the Jungle

Ditching Safe Religion for a Life of Holy Adventure

"It's a dangerous business, Frodo, going out your door. You step onto the road, and if you don't keep your feet, there's no knowing where you might be swept off to."

-Bilbo Baggin, The Lord of the Rings (2001)

Have you ever sensed, deep inside, that your faith was meant to be bigger, braver, and wilder than what you have settled for? If so, you are not alone. We live in a world that constantly tries to shrink God down into something manageable. Faith is often admired as long as it is not disruptive, just enough to keep us respectable and contained. Yet the faith of the Bible the faith that truly pleases God is not careful or controlled. It is daring. Untamed. Alive.

Wild faith is the beating heart of every true adventure with God.

It led Noah to build an ark when rain had never fallen. It moved Moses to face Pharaoh with nothing but a staff and a promise. It stirred Esther to risk her life for the sake of her people. It compelled ordinary fishermen to leave their nets and follow Jesus into the unknown. These were not extraordinary people. They were ordinary people who believed God could do the impossible and then lived as if He would. Wild faith does not begin with confidence. It begins with obedience.

Why do we need wild faith?

Comfort, over time, turns into confinement. What once felt safe slowly becomes a cage. When we remain in the predictable, we miss the life that exists just beyond what feels secure. Familiar routines can quietly dull our hunger for more. Yet it is often in uncertainty that God's transforming power is most clearly revealed.

God's promises are always larger than the plans we construct for ourselves. Our best designs are limited by our perspective, but His plans stretch far beyond what we can imagine. Wild faith dares to believe that every promise from God is an open door into a bolder future. It calls us to release control and trust a divine blueprint greater than anything we could build on our own.

The world is waiting for people who live with this kind of trust. Our time is marked by uncertainty, fear, and exhaustion, and it longs for men and women who act with conviction rooted in God's Word. Wild faith inspires others. It turns ordinary lives into living testimonies. When one person steps forward in bold trust, it creates a ripple that reaches far beyond them.

God is not looking for people who have every answer or every step carefully planned. He is looking for hearts willing to trust Him even when the picture is incomplete. Wild faith prays prayers that stretch beyond logic. It dreams as wide as God's love. It obeys when understanding falls short. This kind of trust reshapes lives, transforms communities, and invites the miraculous into ordinary moments. Wild faith is not reckless. It is surrendered.

What does wild faith look like in real life?

Wild faith rarely shows up in the spotlight. It does not always look impressive to the outside world. In fact, it often looks like tears on the bathroom floor, whispered prayers in the middle of the night, and shaky hands writing checks or stepping onto uncertain ground. It is the kind of faith that bleeds before it blossoms.

It looks like a mother praying in a hospital room over a child doctors say will not survive. Not because she is in denial, but because she knows Jesus is resurrection and life. This is not blind optimism. It is war. It is standing in the impossible and declaring, even now, my God is able.

It looks like choosing forgiveness when it feels unjust. Forgiving a parent who abandoned you. A spouse who betrayed you. A friend who wounded you. Wild faith believes mercy is stronger than bitterness and that restoration is possible even after devastation. It breaks generational cycles by trusting God's justice more than personal revenge.

It looks like saying yes to a calling that makes no earthly sense. Leaving a job. Moving cities. Starting over. Launching a ministry without funding. Returning to school later in life. Writing the book God asked for even when no one else did. Wild faith risks comfort, reputation, and sometimes relationships because it answers to God before fear.

It also looks like staying when leaving would be easier. Holding on to a marriage that feels beyond repair. Choosing counseling. Confessing weakness. Submitting to humility. Trusting that healing is holy even when it is slow.

Wild faith looks like generosity that defies logic. Giving when resources feel scarce because the Spirit whispers, trust Me. It believes in Kingdom provision where small offerings multiply and obedience leads to overflow, even when it comes in unexpected ways.

Wild faith is not heroism. It is surrender. It is choosing God's presence over clarity, His promises over control, and His power over personal strength. It is stepping forward even when you feel weak.

Real wild faith is messy. It will stretch you, break you, heal you, and transform you. It will take you places you never planned to go. And once you have lived it, once you have tasted what it means to trust God beyond sight, you will never want to return to playing it safe. Wild faith is not a moment. It is a way of life. It is how those who walk closely with the King live. It is the posture of those who say, even when I cannot see the whole road, I will follow You thirty-one feet at a time. Wild faith is not recklessness. It is radical trust. It steps forward not because the path is clear, but because the One who leads is faithful.

Wild faith isn't about recklessness; it's about radical trust.

It is knowing that God is bigger than the giants, the storms, and the odds stacked against you. It is stepping out, not because you can see the whole picture, but because you know the One who holds it all.

"Now faith is the substance of things hoped for, the evidence of things not seen."

— Hebrews 11:1

"With man this is impossible, but not with God; all things are possible with God."

— Mark 10:27

"Now to him who is able to do immeasurably more than all we ask or imagine, according to his power that is at work within us..."

— Ephesians 3:20

David: A Shepherd with Wild Faith

He did not look like a warrior. He carried no sword. He was not even old enough to serve in the army. Yet what David had was greater than armor or weapons. He had wild faith.

The battlefield lay in the Valley of Elah. On one side stood the Philistines. On the other stood Israel's army, frozen by fear. For forty days, a giant named Goliath stepped forward, mocking God and intimidating His people. He was massive, heavily armored, and loud. Every soldier saw his size, heard his threats, and ran.

Then David arrived.

He came carrying bread and cheese, sent by his father to check on his brothers. But when he heard Goliath defy the armies of the living God, something ignited inside him. Where others saw danger, David saw an opportunity for God to reveal His glory. He asked the question no one else dared to ask. Who is this uncircumcised Philistine that he should defy the armies of the living God?

His brothers dismissed him. The king doubted him. But David stood firm, not because he was confident in himself, but because he remembered. He remembered the lion. He remembered the bear. He remembered the God who had delivered him before. And he trusted that the same God would deliver him again.

David refused Saul's armor. He was not trying to become someone else. He picked up what he knew. Five smooth stones and a sling. Then he stepped into the valley with intention, not intimidation. He declared to Goliath, you come to me with sword and spear, but I come to you in the name of the Lord of hosts, the God of the armies of Israel. That is wild faith.

It speaks victory before the battle ends. It moves forward without a backup plan. It trusts that God's name is enough when the odds say otherwise. With one stone, David struck the giant down. Not because he was strong, but because he was surrendered. Not because he was fearless, but because his faith outweighed his fear. Not because he saw the whole picture, but because he trusted the One who did.

David's story reminds us that wild faith does not require position, platform, or perfect preparation. It requires a heart that says yes. A heart that believes God still does the impossible. A heart willing to run toward the fight instead of away from it, because it knows who fights with you.

The Cost of Tame Faith

Somewhere along the way, many of us were taught to play it safe with God. Faith became attendance, good behavior, and staying out of trouble. While those things matter, they are not the full picture. Tame faith settles for maintenance when Jesus calls us to movement.

Tame faith never moves mountains. It keeps us on the shore when Jesus is calling us onto the water. It bows to fear and waits until conditions feel right. It says, I will go if everything makes sense. But wild faith says, here I am Lord, send me.

Jesus never invited His followers into a life of comfort. He invited them into a Kingdom where the weak are made strong, the last become first, and obedience often precedes understanding. He called them to deny themselves, take up their cross, and follow Him. That is not a call to safety. It is a call to courage.

The cost of tame faith is subtle but devastating. It shrinks our expectations of God. It replaces dependence with control. Over time, tame faith leaves us spiritually intact but inwardly restless, faithful on the outside yet disconnected on the inside.

Tame faith delays obedience until clarity arrives. Wild faith steps forward trusting that clarity often follows obedience. Tame faith negotiates with fear. Wild faith moves in spite of it. One preserves comfort. The other awakens calling. You can live safely and stay where you are. Or you can follow Jesus into a life that requires trust, surrender, and courage. Faith that never costs you anything will eventually cost you everything.

That is not a call to comfort. That is a call to courage.

My Personal Wilderness

There was a season when my life felt stuck on every front. Relationships were strained. Church felt routine and hollow, full of motion but absent of fire. I was trying to grow closer to God the only way I knew how, yet everything inside me felt dry and unmoving. I had prayed for things that never seemed to change. Dreams I believed were from God stalled or disappeared altogether. Quietly, I began to wonder if this was it. If faith was meant to be managed rather than trusted. If I should stop hoping for more and learn to live safely.

But deep in my spirit, God interrupted that thought with a simple truth. This is not the end. This is the beginning if you will trust Me. That season became the birthplace of a wilder faith. Not faith fueled by outcomes or applause, but faith anchored in obedience. Faith that said yes without knowing what was next. Faith that learned to walk by trust rather than sight.

I discovered that wild faith does not begin with big moments. It begins with small decisions made in hidden places. It is forged in the quiet yes before the door opens. The whispered prayer before provision arrives. The step forward taken before the path is clear. Wild faith is choosing worship when worry feels easier. Showing up in prayer when God feels silent. Forgiving again when the wound still aches. Giving when it makes no sense. Speaking truth when silence feels safer.

These are not dramatic acts. They are deliberate ones. And they are how faith grows strong. This is how Noah kept building. How David kept worshiping. How Ruth kept gleaning. They trusted when it was costly. They obeyed when it was hard. And they found themselves carried into God's unfolding story.

A Wild Invitation

Jesus does not say, "Follow Me to a classroom." He says, "Follow Me." And where He leads is often wild. He leads us off the well-marked path, into places that feel uncertain, unpolished, and demanding. If your life feels like a jungle right now, overgrown, confusing, maybe even dangerous, you may be exactly where He wants you.

You were not made for a sterile version of Christianity. You were made for a faith that breathes, sweats, wrestles, and trusts. The jungle is not your enemy. It is the setting for encounter. It is where faith grows teeth. It is where God proves Himself faithful, not in theory, but in real time.

The jungle is not tidy. There are no neat lines or color-coded maps. Visibility is limited. Control is stripped away. And that is the point. The jungle is not punishment. It is preparation. It is where God dismantles safe religion and builds resilient trust. Where fear is exposed. Where false confidence dies. Where dependence on Him becomes non-negotiable.

In the jungle, God does not usually give you a long-range plan. He gives you Himself. Daily bread. Enough strength for today. Just enough light for the next step. Mystery is not the absence of God here. It is often the doorway to intimacy.

The jungle will change you. That is why it exists. Not to break you, but to form you. Not to delay you, but to deepen you. Those who walk through it do not come out with answers for everything. They come out with a faith that no longer depends on safety, certainty, or control, but on the unshakable faithfulness of God. If you want safe, you can stay where you are. If you want sacred, you will follow the voice calling you deeper.

What You'll Find in the Jungle

The jungle is not a place of ease. It is a place of encounter. It is where faith stops being theory and God becomes personal. Predictability is stripped away and replaced with presence. Here, God is no longer a concept you study. He becomes the One you follow.

In the jungle, you will not receive a detailed map. God rarely offers long-range plans here. Instead, He offers Himself. As clarity fades, dependence deepens. Mystery is not the absence of God. It is often the doorway to intimacy.

You will face resistance. Fear rises. Doubt surfaces. Weariness sets in. But resistance is not proof that you are off course. More often, it is confirmation that you are exactly where God is working. The jungle is where courage is formed and comfort loses its authority.

The jungle transforms you. It exposes where control replaced trust and comfort replaced calling. What is unnecessary is stripped away. Not to destroy you, but to rebuild you. Something must die here. Fear. Pride. The need to have everything figured out. And in its place, something stronger is born.

You will find provision in the jungle, even when it looks like scarcity. Daily bread. Enough strength for today. Just enough light for the next step. God may not remove the jungle, but He will never abandon you in it. And above all, you will find Jesus. Not the distant version learned in safe spaces, but the living King who walks with you through the wild.

The jungle will change you. That is the point. It is not punishment. It is preparation. Those who walk through it emerge with a faith no longer dependent on safety, certainty, or control, but anchored in the unshakable faithfulness of God.

The Point of Change

There comes a moment in the jungle when something shifts inside you. It is rarely loud. There is no lightning or spectacle. It happens quietly, almost unnoticed, but nothing is the same afterward.

The point of change arrives when you stop asking God for escape and begin asking Him for endurance. When you stop pleading for the wilderness to end and start trusting Him within it. What once felt like punishment begins to feel like preparation.

You begin to see that the waiting was not wasted. The struggle was not pointless. God was not trying to break you. He was building something in you that could only be formed under pressure. Roots were growing deeper. Vision was sharpening. Strength was being forged where comfort once ruled.

At the point of change, your identity loosens its grip on performance and approval and anchors itself in who God says you are. Faith matures from borrowed belief into lived conviction. It is no longer inherited or assumed. It is tested, personal, and real.

You begin to walk with a quieter confidence. Not because everything is clear, but because you have encountered God in the wild. You have seen Him provide when you had nothing. You have felt His presence when others walked away. You have been carried when your strength failed. And now you know. He is not only the God of mountaintops. He is the God of the jungle.

That knowledge changes how you live. You are no longer afraid of the unknown because you have met God there. Faith stops being something you visit and becomes the way you walk. This book is an invitation to live from that place.

This book is an invitation to step forward even when you cannot see what comes next. Wild faith does not require a full map, only a willing heart. Like the rhino that can only see thirty feet ahead, you were never meant to wait for perfect clarity. You were created to trust God for the next step.

The thirty-first foot is where fear loses its voice and faith finds its strength. It is where obedience moves before understanding and trust outruns sight. You may not see the whole road, but you can see far enough to move. And when you take that step, God will meet you there. This is not a guide to safe religion. It is a call to live forward. One faithful step. One bold yes. Thirty-one feet at a time.

Coaching Insight

The Big Truth

Wild faith begins where safe religion ends. God does not call us to manage belief, but to trust Him beyond what feels controllable, predictable, or secure.

The Mirror Question

Where in your life have you chosen safety over surrender?
What might God be inviting you to trust Him with that you have been trying to control?

The Thirty First Footstep

Identify one place in your life where obedience has been delayed because clarity feels incomplete. Acknowledge the next faithful step God is inviting you to take, even if you cannot yet see beyond it.

The Inner Work

Entering the jungle of faith often awakens fear before it strengthens trust. This does not mean you are failing. It means something real is happening. Allow yourself to notice what surfaces without judgment. God does some of His deepest work in the places where control loosens and dependence grows.

Reflection Prompt

What emotions or physical responses arise as you consider stepping forward in trust? Where do you notice resistance or hesitation within yourself?

Prayer of Alignment

Jesus, I release my need for certainty and control. I choose to trust You beyond what I can see. Meet me in this place of surrender and give me courage to move forward in obedience. I place my confidence not in my understanding, but in Your faithfulness. Amen.

CHAPTER 2:
NO MORE CAGES

What Happens When Faith Breaks Free

"We are all in cages with the door wide open"

- George Lucas

Wild faith always costs something. If Chapter One was an invitation into the wild, this chapter names what must be left behind. Because no one steps fully into freedom without first confronting the cages they have learned to live in.

Most cages are not built overnight. They are formed slowly, quietly, and often with good intentions. They begin as protection. Wisdom. Survival. But over time, what once kept us safe becomes what keeps us stuck. Cages rarely look like rebellion. More often, they look like routine. They sound like this:

"This is just how I am."
"This is as far as I can go."
"This is realistic."
"This is wise."

Wild faith hears something different. It hears God calling us beyond what feels reasonable and into what requires trust. The tragedy is not that we have limits. The tragedy is when we mistake limits for calling.

Many of us learned to live inside invisible bars. Fear shaped them. Disappointment reinforced them. Pain justified them. Over time, we adjusted our expectations to fit the space we were willing to occupy. We prayed safer prayers. We dreamed smaller dreams. We told ourselves we were being mature, when in reality, we were being cautious with a God who is anything but cautious.

Jesus never invited anyone to improve their cage. He invited them to leave it.

He did not say refine your comfort or manage your fear. He said, follow Me. And following Him always requires movement. It always involves release. Something must be left behind.

For some, the cage is fear of failure. For others, it is the need for approval. For many, it is disappointment with God that was never fully spoken aloud. These cages are reinforced every time we choose familiarity over obedience. The most dangerous cages are the ones we stop noticing. They feel normal. Predictable. Manageable. But wild faith cannot grow where movement is restricted.

Freedom always begins with awareness.

The moment you recognize the bars, you are already closer to the door.

This chapter is not about guilt. It is about honesty. It is about naming what has confined you so it no longer controls you. God does not expose cages to shame us. He reveals them to lead us out.

No more cages does not mean reckless living. It means surrendered living. It means refusing to call captivity wisdom and refusing to settle for a faith that never stretches you. Wild faith cannot live behind bars. And neither were you created to.

Let's get real. Wild faith is rare, even in the church. We often celebrate stories of faith in others, but quietly keep our own belief contained within the borders of what feels possible or predictable. Wild faith, however, is different. It is faith that refuses to stay in the lines. It does not settle for safe. It does not ask permission to believe. And when it breaks free, it changes everything.

Wild faith is not about hype. It is not shallow optimism or some spiritual adrenaline rush. Wild faith is forged in the fire, in delay, disappointment, and unanswered prayers. It grows roots in dry ground and lifts its voice in storms. It is the kind of faith that still believes when the door has not opened, when the healing has not come, when the path is not clear. It is gritty. It is stubborn in the best way. And it is powerful because it is anchored not in outcomes, but in the nature of God Himself.

Wild faith is:

Untamed by disappointment. It is easy to trust God when everything goes as planned. But wild faith is different. It shows up when life falls apart. It worships when the heart is broken. It clings to hope when the outcome is uncertain. Wild faith does not deny pain. It endures it. It does not pretend everything is fine. It refuses to stop trusting God in the middle of the mess.

Unchained by logic. Wild faith sees reality, but it responds to revelation. It acknowledges what is hard, but it listens to the voice of the One who calls us beyond what we can see. Wild faith does not mean you stop thinking. It means you stop letting fear and logic be the final authority. It believes that the God who parted seas and raised the dead can still do the impossible.

Unashamed to act. Wild faith does not just agree with God. It obeys Him. It does not live in the theoretical. It steps into the real. It moves when God says move, even when it is scary, even when it costs. It walks across the street, makes the phone call, forgives the wound, gives the gift, prays the prayer, and takes the leap. Wild faith does not always feel ready, but it chooses obedience anyway.

Wild Faith in Scripture

Abraham: God told him, "Go… to the land I will show you" (Genesis 12:1). No map. No GPS. No guarantees. Just a promise. Abraham left everything familiar because he believed that God would be faithful to lead him. Wild faith means walking even when you do not know the destination, because you trust the One who is leading.

Joshua and Caleb: When the ten other spies returned full of fear, they stood with boldness. "We are well able to overcome it," they declared (Numbers 13:30). Wild faith sees the giants but focuses on the

God who is bigger. It does not minimize reality. It magnifies God's ability.

The Woman with the Issue of Blood: Twelve years of suffering. Twelve years of being overlooked, outcast, and forgotten. Yet she pressed through the crowd, believing that just one touch of Jesus could change everything. Wild faith does not let obstacles stop it. It moves through pain, past opinions, and beyond resistance, because it knows Jesus is worth reaching for.

Every one of these stories carries the same truth. Wild faith moves before certainty arrives.

What Wild Faith Looks Like Today

Wild faith in today's world is just as radical as it was in Scripture. It might not involve parting a sea, but it may look like starting a business that honors God, even when the economy says no. It may look like trusting for a miracle when doctors have given up hope. It may look like opening your home to foster care or adoption when your life already feels full. It may look like forgiving a betrayal that shattered your heart. It may look like leaving a secure job to step into your God-given calling.

Wild faith today means choosing to believe God in the everyday and in the extraordinary. It is choosing love over fear, generosity over scarcity, and surrender over control. It is a willingness to go first, to speak truth, to carry peace, and to live as if Jesus is enough.

History also gives us echoes of wild, untamed faith, even outside the pages of Scripture.

One such story is that of Florence Nightingale. She was born into privilege and expectation. Her future was carefully planned for her. Marriage. Status. Comfort. But she believed God had called her to something else. Against the resistance of her family and the norms of her time, she obeyed that calling and stepped into the suffering of others. During the Crimean War, she cared for wounded soldiers in filthy, overcrowded hospitals, often working through the night by lamplight. She did not fight with weapons or speeches. She fought neglect, apathy, and fear with obedience and compassion. Nightingale once said she stood at a crossroads and chose the path of obedience to God. Her wild faith refused the cage of expectation and changed the course of modern medicine.

Harriet Tubman escaped slavery but returned again and again to lead others out, trusting God step by step through danger and darkness.

Dietrich Bonhoeffer resisted a corrupted church and a violent regime, choosing costly obedience over safe silence.

Corrie ten Boom hid the persecuted, endured imprisonment, and later forgave her enemies, proving that love can outlast hatred.

Their lives remind us that wild faith does not only liberate individuals. It frees others.

"Despite all my rage, I am still just a rat in a cage."

The Smashing Pumpkins, Bullet with Butterfly Wings

One morning, I was in the gym working out, listening to a random playlist filled with 1990s pop music. I had been working on this chapter the night before, praying, pondering, and writing about what it means to break free from the cages that keep our faith contained. That is when the lyrics hit me. "Despite all my rage, I am still just a rat in a cage."

Sweat dripping, headphones on, weights clanking around me, and suddenly I was no longer in the gym. I was back inside old patterns I thought I had outgrown. Childhood memories flooded my mind. Days of inner turmoil. Moments of anger I could not explain. Seasons where my faith felt more like performance than freedom. It felt as though God had reached through the music and confirmed something I could not shake. This song needed to be part of the story.

This lyric captures a brutal truth many feel but rarely say out loud. The ache of spiritual frustration. The torment of being trapped in cycles of sin, shame, or stagnancy, even while yearning for something more. It is the voice of a soul locked inside religion without relationship, routine without renewal. It screams of a man-made cage that even passion cannot unlock. In many ways, this song echoes the cry of the restless heart, angry, disillusioned, worn down by the pretense of freedom while still feeling stuck. And yet…

The story does not have to end that way.

While the band's lyrics culminate in despair, the Gospel leads to deliverance. Jesus specializes in opening cages, spiritual, emotional, and mental, and in setting captives free. Even when it feels like the rage within us will never subside, God's mercy still breaks in. Yes, you may feel like a rat in a cage. Yes, the rage may feel real. But no, that is not where your story must end.

Wild faith breaks the cycle. It tears through bars of bitterness. It climbs past the echo of disappointment. It says, "There is more. I was made for more."

Common Misconceptions About Wild Faith

"Wild faith is reckless." Not true. Wild faith is not careless or impulsive. It is deeply rooted in God's Word and character. It does not chase emotions. It chases obedience. It is not jumping for a thrill. It is stepping where God leads, no matter the cost.

"Wild faith is for special people." Also, false. God never reserved faith for a spiritual elite. Wild faith is not about personality or position. It is about a willing heart that says, "Here I am, Lord. Send me."

"Wild faith means no doubt." Even the heroes of faith had moments of uncertainty. What makes their stories powerful is not their perfection, but their persistence. Wild faith does not mean you never waver. It means that even in your wavering, you keep walking.

When wild faith breaks free, something shifts. Fear loses its grip. Chains fall off. You stop waiting for the perfect moment and start trusting the perfect God. You realize faith is not just something you have. It is something you unleash. And once it is loose, there is no going back.

So let this be the moment. No more cages. No more small, polite belief. The world does not need more safe Christians. It needs people of holy fire. People of divine daring. People of wild, untamed, break-the-mold kind of faith.

And that, my friend, can be you.

Coaching Insight

The Big Truth

Wild faith always costs something. God does not call us to decorate our cages, but to recognize them and walk out when He opens the door.

The Mirror Question

What cage have you learned to live in that God may be inviting you to leave behind? Where have fear, disappointment, or logic quietly shaped the limits of your faith?

The Thirty First Foot Step

Identify one belief, habit, or pattern that has kept your faith contained. Name the next faithful step that would require trust rather than control, even if it feels uncomfortable or costly.

The Inner Work

Leaving a cage often stirs resistance before relief. Fear may speak loudly. Old narratives may try to pull you back toward what feels familiar. This does not mean you are wrong. It often means you are finally becoming honest. God meets us not after we escape, but as we begin to loosen our grip on what once felt safe.

Reflection Prompt

What emotions surface as you imagine stepping beyond this limitation? Where do you feel tension, hesitation, or grief in your body or thoughts?

Prayer of Alignment

Jesus, I confess that I have learned to live within limits You never set for me. I release fear, disappointment, and control into Your hands. Give me courage to leave what has confined me and trust You beyond what feels safe. Lead me into the freedom You have already prepared. I choose obedience over comfort and trust over fear. Amen.

Chapter 3:
Born for the Wild

Faith that Moves Before Clarity

"The meaning of life is not simply to exist, but to move ahead, to go up, to achieve, to conquer."

— Arnold Schwarzenegger

Imagine standing at the edge of a vast African savanna as the morning sun breaks the horizon, pouring gold across miles of untamed land. The air is crisp, carrying the scent of earth and possibility.

In the distance, a rhinoceros stands still, muscles coiled, skin marked by years of weather and survival. Its ears swivel. Its nostrils flare. Then, without hesitation, it charges forward. Dust rises. The ground trembles. It does not know what lies beyond its limited vision. Danger or opportunity. Resistance or open ground. But it moves anyway. Not recklessly. Confidently. Because it was created for the wild.

Now imagine that same rhino behind glass and concrete in a city zoo. Its strength remains, but its world has shrunk. Familiar paths. Timed meals. Predictable routines. Visitors watch from a safe distance as it paces the same worn circle again and again. Alive, but contained. Existing, but not thriving.

The tragedy is not that the zoo's rhino is weak. It is that over time, it forgets what it was built for.

Muscles designed for miles adapt to circles. Instincts sharpened for survival grow dull. Power becomes ornamental instead of functional. The rhino is still strong. Its strength is simply no longer required. Both rhinos were born with the same strength. Only one is fully alive. God did not design your faith for a cage.

Escaping the Comfort Trap

You were created to trust Him beyond what you can see. To follow Him into places that stretch you. To live a faith that moves before clarity arrives. Yet over time, disappointment, fear, and the desire for safety can tame our faith until we find ourselves pacing spiritual enclosures. Our prayers become careful. Our obedience becomes conditional. Our passion grows quiet. Like the zoo rhino, we may feel protected, but we are no longer fully alive.

Comfort is not evil, but it can become a spiritual anesthetic. When faith is shaped by convenience and predictability, dependence on God slowly fades. A faith that requires no risk soon becomes a faith that requires no God at all.

I have sat across from people who loved God deeply but felt quietly confined by comfort. One man shared how he felt stuck in a career that paid well but slowly hollowed him out. He sensed God stirring something new, but the fear of instability kept him frozen. Every prayer sounded the same. Lord, show me more before I move. What he really wanted was assurance without surrender.

Another woman described feeling called toward a space far beyond her qualifications. She assumed confidence would come first. Instead, the invitation kept coming while uncertainty remained. Her faith began to move only when obedience outweighed her need to feel ready.

Neither stepped forward because it felt safe. They stepped forward because staying contained began to feel more costly than trusting God. Jesus never called His followers into ease. He called them to surrender. Follow Me. Take up your cross. Leave the boat. Obedience has always required movement. Something must be released before something new can be received.

Moving With a Newborn and No Blueprint

There was a season when God invited our family into something that made very little sense on paper. We had just welcomed our first baby into the world. Life felt sacred and fragile. Sleep was thin. Emotions were close. The weight of fatherhood had just settled onto my shoulders. Every decision carried consequences. And that is when the stirring began. Tennessee. Plant a church.

It was not dramatic. No lightning bolt. No audible voice. Just a quiet, persistent nudge that would not leave. I remember holding our newborn and whispering, Lord, now?

We had diapers to buy. A family to stabilize. A rhythm to build. Church planting felt disruptive, not logical. Not to mention that my wife was not particularly on board with the idea at the time.

When you are newly married, risk feels shared. When you are new parents, risk feels amplified.

What if I cannot provide?
What if this creates instability for my wife?
What if I mishear God and my family pays the price?

My wife and I talked late into the night between feedings and exhaustion. We did not want adventure. We wanted obedience. One day while we were making our bed together, out of nowhere, she quietly said, "If this is God, I would rather trust Him in the unknown than stay somewhere safe without Him."

That sentence settled something in us. We prayed for clarity. Instead, we received peace that did not erase uncertainty. The door was not flung open. It was barely cracked. Just enough light for the next step. And that was all we were given. One step.

Packing boxes with a newborn in the next room felt holy and terrifying at the same time. After we arrived in Tennessee, reality settled in. Finances were lean. Momentum was slow. There were nights I walked quietly through our apartment after everyone was asleep, praying in whispers. God, did I lead us here correctly? The vulnerability stripped away self-reliance. But something deeper grew. Dependence.

We saw a provision we could not manufacture. We experienced the nearness of God in ways comfort never would have required. Clarity did not precede the move. The voice did. And sometimes the voice is enough.

One of the clearest pictures of this is Peter stepping out of the boat. Surrounded by wind and waves, he heard a single word from Jesus. Come. Peter did not wait for calmer water or a clearer plan. He stepped out. He walked. He faltered. And he was caught. Wild faith does not mean flawless faith. It means willing faith. It is better to step out and stumble than to stay seated and never move.

Throughout Scripture, God consistently moves through people who respond before clarity arrives. Abraham left without a map. Esther spoke before safety was guaranteed. David ran toward a giant while others retreated. Obedience came first. Understanding followed later.

In a tucked-away corner of Scripture, we meet a man named Benaiah. On a snowy day, he chased a lion into a pit and killed it. No witnesses. No applause. No safety net. Just a decision to move when fear said wait. God remembered that moment. It became a defining marker in Benaiah's life and led to greater responsibility and trust. Faith does not wait for ideal conditions. It responds to holy invitation.

I have watched this same pattern unfold in real lives. A couple choosing counseling when pride urged them to walk away. A parent forgiving wounds that still ached because bitterness had become its own cage. A leader stepping into a calling they never planned for because staying comfortable began to feel more dangerous than trusting God.

None of these moments looked dramatic from the outside. There were no spotlights or applause. Just quiet decisions made in uncertain spaces. But those decisions became turning points. Faith did not wait for clarity. It moved because God was already present in the step.

Before we ever live caged lives outwardly, we agree to them inwardly. Internal narratives shaped by fear and past wounds quietly become bars. I am not enough. It is too late. Others are more qualified. God probably will not move. These are not just thoughts. They are cages.

The Cage of Mental Distortion

Many of the limits we live with are not imposed by circumstances, people, or opportunity. They are formed by thought patterns shaped over time by fear, disappointment, and pain. Scripture calls this the battleground of the mind. These internal cages often sound reasonable. They feel logical. They present themselves as wisdom. But they quietly shape decisions, restrict obedience, and shrink faith.

The apostle Paul tells us that we are transformed by the renewing of our minds. This is not positive thinking. It is spiritual alignment. It is learning to stop agreeing with fear and start agreeing with truth.

Below are some of the most common mental cages and the truths that dismantle them.

Limiting Belief: If I fail, I will be rejected

God's Truth: Nothing can separate me from the love of God. Romans 8:39

For many, this belief did not begin in adulthood. It formed in early experiences where approval felt conditional, and performance equaled belonging. When faith invites risk, the old fear rises. Failure is no longer about outcome. It feels like abandonment.

But the gospel dismantles this entirely. You are not loved because you succeed. You are loved because you are His. Obedience does not secure your acceptance. It flows from it.

Limiting Belief: If I cannot do it perfectly, I should not try

God's Truth: God's grace is sufficient, and His power is made perfect in weakness. 2 Corinthians 12:9

Perfectionism often disguises itself as excellence. But underneath it is fear. If it cannot be flawless, it feels unsafe. So we delay. We overprepare. We wait until we feel ready.

But readiness is rarely the prerequisite for calling. Weakness is.

God does not ask for polish. He asks for surrender. Waiting until you feel perfect is often another way of waiting forever.

Limiting Belief: Others are more qualified than me

God's Truth: God often chooses the unlikely and the overlooked. 1 Corinthians 1:27

Comparison is a subtle cage. It whispers that someone else is better equipped, more experienced, more spiritual. It sounds humble, but it quietly removes responsibility.

Throughout Scripture, God consistently calls people who feel underqualified. Moses stuttered. Gideon hid. David was overlooked. Peter doubted.

The question is rarely, are you the most qualified?
The question is, are you willing?

Availability often matters more than ability.

Limiting Belief: If God has not moved yet, maybe He never will

God's Truth: God's promises unfold in His appointed time. Habakkuk 2:3

Delay can feel like denial. Silence can feel like absence. When prayers seem unanswered, the mind begins to create conclusions.

Maybe I misheard Him.
Maybe I asked for too much.
Maybe this will never happen.

But waiting seasons are often formation seasons. God's timing is not indifferent. It is intentional. He is shaping capacity while you wait. The absence of movement is not the absence of God.

These distortions loosen their grip when they are exposed to truth and met with obedience. Truth alone informs. Truth acted upon transforms.

Every time you choose trust over fear, a bar bends. Every time you move forward in faith, a door opens wider. Freedom is rarely one dramatic breakthrough. It is repeated agreements with truth in moments that feel small.

Sometimes the most dangerous cages are spiritual ones.

Routine without risk.
Religion without movement.
Faith that looks respectable but carries no power.

You can attend church faithfully and still live contentedly. You can speak Christian language and still be governed by fear. Jesus never modeled safe belief. His presence disrupted systems. His obedience offended comfort. He crossed boundaries, overturned tables, and called ordinary people into costly faith. He still does.

Escaping comfort is not only about personal growth. It is about calling. You were not saved to sit. You were saved to be sent. Across the street or across the world. Into the difficult conversation or the unseen assignment.

Faith that moves before clarity does not rely on certainty. It relies on the character of God. Somewhere beyond comfort, the Kingdom is waiting. Somewhere beyond certainty, God is already at work. You were not made for the enclosure. You were not created for the cage. You were born for the wild.

Coaching Insight

The Big Truth

You were created for obedience, not safety. Wild faith moves before clarity because trust is anchored in who God is, not in how much you can see.

The Mirror Question

Where has comfort quietly replaced obedience in your life? What step might God be inviting you to take that feels uncertain but faithful?

The Thirty-First Foot Step

Name one place where you have been waiting for clarity before moving. Acknowledge the next faithful step God is inviting you to take, even if the outcome remains unknown.

The Inner Work

Stepping beyond comfort often awakens fear and old narratives that say stay safe. These voices are familiar, but they are not authoritative. God often meets us not after certainty arrives, but in the act of trusting Him without it.

Reflection Prompt

What thoughts or emotions surface as you imagine stepping forward without guarantees? Where do you notice resistance within yourself?

Prayer of Alignment

Jesus, I release my need to see the whole path before I move. I choose to trust You beyond what feels safe or predictable. Strengthen my heart to obey when clarity feels incomplete. I place my confidence in Your character and Your presence. Lead me forward, one faithful step at a time. Amen.

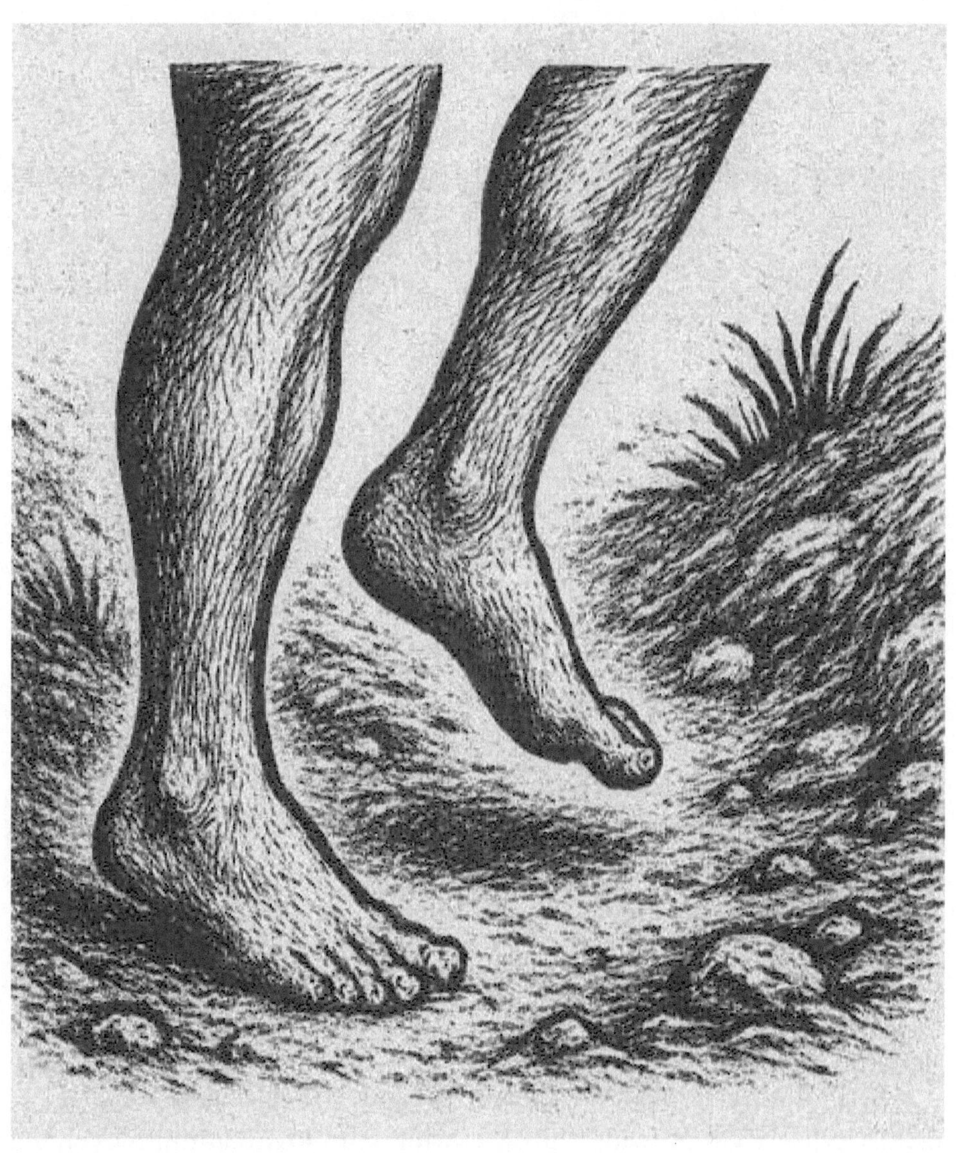

CHAPTER 4:
RUNNING WILD

Real Stories of Daring Faith in Motion

"Do not go where the path may lead, go instead where there is no path and leave a trail."

— Ralph Waldo Emerson

Faith is not a theory. It is a living story. Yours. Mine. God's people through the ages. Scripture is not a museum of heroes. It is a blueprint for movement. Faith that stays still will not stay strong. From the moment Jesus said, "Follow Me," faith became an invitation to motion. It was never meant to sit idle or remain parked inside what feels familiar.

When God calls, you go.
When God speaks, you move.
When God stirs your heart, you run.

Running faith is not frantic. It is intentional. It moves toward obedience even when clarity lags. It runs because hunger is stronger than comfort. We were born to run.

We were born to run, not aimlessly, not frantically, but full of holy purpose. Born to run toward calling. Born to run past fear. Born to run into divine adventure. As Olympic runner Eric Liddell famously said in the film *Chariots of Fire*, "God made me fast. And when I run, I feel His pleasure." That line isn't just about speed; it's about purpose. When we run in alignment with the way God designed us. Whether in ministry, creativity, service, or leadership, we bring Him joy. Faithful movement is not just obedience; it's worship in motion. It's saying with every step, "I was born to do this, and You, God, are my delight."

Ralph Waldo Emerson's quote, "Do not go where the path may lead; go instead where there is no path and leave a trail." That single sentence captures the heart of wild faith.

Running with God has never been about staying on marked paths or following well-worn trails. It has always been about movement into places where clarity is limited, and obedience must come first. Faith does not wait for certainty. It creates holy momentum by trusting God step by step, even when the ground ahead feels unfamiliar.

Wild faith runs where there is no path yet because it trusts the One who walks ahead. Running faith is fueled by hunger.

In his book *The God Chasers*, Tommy Tenney writes, "A God chaser is a person whose hunger exceeds his reach. He's desperate to touch the heart of God." This kind of desperation isn't born out of boredom or routine; it's born out of holy restlessness. God chasers are not content to live off yesterday's manna. They long for fresh fire, fresh presence, and fresh direction.

Faith that runs real, daring, risk-taking faith is fueled by hunger. The more you chase God, the more He invites you deeper. Hunger keeps people moving when comfort says settle. Hungry faith does not wait for perfect conditions. Moses cried, "Show me Your glory." David said, "My soul thirsts for You." Hunger refuses to live on yesterday's manna.

Hunger is what separates passive belief from passionate pursuit. It's what drives people to wake early to pray, to linger long in worship, to study the Word not for information but for transformation. Hunger is what makes you weep over a verse you've read a hundred times, because this time, God speaks through it directly to your heart.

Spiritual hunger is not a luxury for the emotionally expressive; it's the lifeblood of the disciple. Jesus said, "Blessed are those who hunger and thirst for righteousness, for they will be filled" (Matthew 5:6). The promise is clear: if you hunger, He will fill. But if you settle, if you get comfortable in yesterday's revelation or someone else's fire, you may miss what He's doing right in front of you. Hunger draws you into places others won't go. It makes you sensitive to the Spirit's whisper and bold in the face of apathy. Hungry people don't need hype; they burn from the inside out.

To run with God is to hunger for Him daily, not just for what He can do, but for who He is. The kind of pursuit that makes you change your plans, surrender your comfort, and chase after the One thing that matters most: Him. This hunger becomes a holy ache, a longing that doesn't disappear with a single encounter. It deepens. It intensifies. It keeps you coming back, even after you've seen miracles or felt His presence. You want more, not because He's holding back, but because He's infinite. The more you taste, the more you want. The more you want, the stronger the yearn.

It's the yearning that keeps you kneeling long after the song has ended. It's what keeps you trusting when your prayers haven't been answered. It's the fire that refuses to die down, even when the world grows cold.

Yearning for God is what sustains the long run of faith. It's what anchors you when the steps of obedience become steep, and the road of calling gets lonely. It's not about spiritual excitement; it's about sacred dependency. It's saying, "God, I can't pursue You. Nothing else satisfies."

Because once you've tasted His nearness, once you've glimpsed His glory, nothing else compares. Your soul begins to echo David's cry in

Psalm 63:1: "O God, You are my God; earnestly I seek You; my soul thirsts for You, my flesh faints for You, as in a dry and weary land where there is no water."

This is what it means to run, not for applause, not for answers, but for Him.

Jesus promised that those who hunger and thirst will be filled. Hungry faith does not need hype. It burns from the inside out. This is the faith that runs.

Running Faith in Scripture

Joshua and Caleb saw the same giants as everyone else, but they remembered a bigger God. While fear paralyzed the crowd, Caleb said, "Let us go up at once." Running faith remembers what God has already done and moves forward anyway.

A Roman centurion trusted Jesus without needing proximity or proof. "Just say the word," he said. Jesus marveled. Running faith trusts the authority of God's word even from a distance.

A woman who had bled for twelve years pushed through a crowd with no invitation and no guarantee. One reach changed everything. Running faith does not wait for permission. It reaches.

Peter stepped out of the boat while the storm still raged. He faltered. He was caught. The miracle was not walking on water. It was discovering that Jesus was close enough to rescue him when he sank.

Shadrach, Meshach, and Abednego stood firm with no promise of rescue. "Even if He does not…" That is wild faith. Obedience without conditions.

Eleazar stood his ground when everyone else ran. He fought for a field that fed people. Running faith holds ground when retreat would be easier.

Every one of them moved before knowing the outcome. That is what makes faith wild.

What Makes This Faith Wild

Wild faith is not reckless.

It is responsive.

It does not eliminate fear.

It obeys in the presence of fear.

It runs toward God rather than away from discomfort.

It trusts character more than outcomes.

Faith grows in motion.

Hunger keeps it moving.

Obedience gives it direction.

How Do I Learn to Run with My Faith?

Running with faith is not something you master all at once. It is learned the same way running itself is learned, one step, one breath, one mile at a time. You do not wake up one day suddenly fearless, decisive, and bold. You become those things by moving before you feel ready.

Most people believe they will run once confidence arrives. Scripture teaches the opposite. Confidence grows because we run.

Learning to run with your faith begins with responding to God in small, ordinary moments. The conversation you feel prompted to have. The prayer you sense you should pray. The generosity that stretches you. The obedience that feels inconvenient. These moments may not look heroic, but they train your spiritual muscles. Faith grows strong through use.

Running faith also requires learning to recognize God's voice. Not every voice urging movement is from God. But his voice is consistent. It aligns with Scripture. It produces peace even when it creates discomfort. It invites trust rather than fear-driven urgency. As you obey in small things, discernment sharpens. You begin to recognize His tone. His timing. His direction. You learn to run by learning to listen.

Running faith also means learning to tolerate uncertainty. Faith does not remove unanswered questions. It teaches you to carry them without stopping. Most callings unfold while clarity lags behind obedience. God often reveals the next step only after the previous one is taken. You are not failing because you feel unsure. You are learning to run.

Another part of learning to run is accepting that fear will travel with you. Fear does not disappear when faith is real. It simply loses authority. Courage is not the absence of fear. It is obedience that refuses to let fear decide. Running faith says, I am afraid, but I am moving anyway.

Finally, learning to run requires trust in God's character more than trust in your capacity. You will not always feel strong. You will not always feel prepared. You will not always feel certain. But God is faithful. He does not ask you to outrun Him. He asks you to follow. You learn to run by trusting that He keeps pace with you.

Faith is not learned by standing still and thinking harder. It is learned by stepping forward and discovering that God meets you there. That is how runners are formed. Not in theory. But in motion.

Running Faith Today

Wild faith did not end in Scripture. I have watched it run through ordinary people whose obedience carried extraordinary weight.

Jimmy Wayne once ran for survival. Homeless as a teenager, passed between systems and shadows, he learned what it meant to live unseen. Years later, with a guitar on his back and conviction in his chest, he walked more than a thousand miles so foster children would be seen and heard. He ran because someone once opened a door for him, and faith would not let him forget the ones still waiting behind gates.

Bryan and Haley Jarrett chose obedience that made no financial sense. They served a struggling church without pay, trusting God day by day for provision. When the year ended, Bryan entered a season of fasting and silence, desperate for direction. Alone in a cabin, physically weak and spiritually hungry, God met him through an unexpected stranger sent to deliver a word at the exact moment he needed it. Running faith listens long enough to hear heaven speak.

Rick and Denise Renner left a thriving life in Tulsa, Oklahoma, and moved their family to post-Soviet Russia. No language. No certainty. No safety net. They stayed through cold winters, scarcity, and isolation. Decades later, their obedience has shaped leaders, churches, and nations. Running faith keeps going when comfort is no longer an option.

Winston Bui fled war as a child and later encountered Jesus as a teenager searching for identity and belonging. Choosing faith created tension and uncertainty, but he kept running. Today, he carries the Gospel to displaced and forgotten people across borders. Running faith redeems what was broken and sends it back out with purpose.

None of these people felt ready. All of them felt called.

Running faith does not wait until the path is clear. It moves because God is already present in the step. You were not created to circle the same ground forever. You were made to run. Not aimlessly. Not recklessly. But boldly toward the voice of God.

Someone is waiting on the other side of your obedience. There is a future that will not unfold until you take the next step. God is not looking for the most polished or prepared. He is looking for the willing. Wild faith does not sit still. It runs.

My Prayer of Blessing Over You

As I write these words, I am praying this blessing over you, trusting that God will meet you in the moment you read them, whether it is days or years from now.

May you run with holy hunger that refuses to settle for less than God's presence.

May you run with courage that moves even when clarity has not yet arrived.

May you run with trust that God is already ahead of you, preparing the way step by step.

May you run free from the weight of fear, comparison, and hesitation.

May you run with endurance when the path grows long, and the cost feels heavy.

May you run with joy, knowing that obedience is never wasted and faith is never unseen.

May you run not for applause or certainty, but for the pleasure of the One who called you.

And when you stumble, may you discover that Jesus is close enough to catch you.

May your life become a trail of faith others can follow.

May you run, not away from the wild places, but straight into them, confident that God is with you. Amen.

Coaching Insight

The Big Truth

Faith grows through movement. Hunger fuels obedience, and obedience releases momentum.

The Mirror Question

Where has your faith slowed into routine? What invitation from God have you sensed but delayed?

The Thirty-First Foot Step

Name the next faithful action God may be inviting you to take. Do not wait for certainty. Move with trust.

The Inner Work

Resistance often appears just before movement matters most. Fear does not mean stop. It often means go.

Reflection Prompt

What stirs inside you when you imagine running toward obedience rather than waiting for clarity?

Prayer of Alignment

Jesus, awaken holy hunger within me. I choose movement over comfort and obedience over certainty. Strengthen me to run toward You even when the path is unclear. Lead me forward, one faithful step at a time. Amen.

CHAPTER 5: FAITH ON FIRE

Ignition Point: When the Ordinary Sparks the Extraordinary

"Set yourself on fire, and people will come from miles to watch you burn."

-John Wesley

Fire, in its most basic sense, is a chemical reaction called combustion, a process in which fuel rapidly combines with oxygen in the presence of heat, producing light, warmth, and energy. But if you remove just one of these three components, fuel, oxygen, or heat, the flame cannot survive.

Fuel + Oxygen → Carbon Dioxide + Water + Heat (Energy)

Yet fire is far more than a natural phenomenon. For millennia, it has fascinated, frightened, and inspired people. It gives warmth in the cold, light in darkness, and power to transform raw materials into something new. Fire can be destructive, but it is also deeply creative, a force that brings change, refines, and purifies.

Early humans would travel miles to bring fire back to their camps. Entire rituals were built around keeping it alive. Sparks were preserved through storms and migrations. Embers were carried in pots. Losing fire was not merely inconvenient. It was dangerous. Even today, we feel its pull. There is something mesmerizing about it, something alive in the flicker of a flame. It dances. It breathes. It consumes. And it speaks a language deeper than words.

To watch a flame is to witness transformation in real time. It is no wonder that throughout history, fire has marked beginnings: the first light at dawn, the first campfire of a new settlement, the first strike of flint against steel. It is the ignition point, not only of survival, but of civilization.

Long before cities rose and languages divided, before scrolls were written or wheels were turned, fire stood at the center. Anthropologists trace the earliest controlled use of fire back nearly 1.5 million years ago, in the cradle of Africa, at a site called Koobi Fora along the eastern shore of Lake Turkana. There, among stone tools and scattered bones, scientists discovered darkened earth and burnt fragments, evidence of ancient hearths. Not wildfires. Not accidents. These were fires that had been tended, protected, and used.

Imagine it.

A group of early humans huddled beneath the stars, the first sparks of fire crackling in front of them. The darkness held unknown predators. The cold pressed in without mercy. But in the glow of that fire, something began to shift. Not just temperature. Not just visibility. Identity. Community. Intention. Around fire, we did not simply survive. We began to speak. We started to share stories, shape tools, cook food, and create culture. Fire slowed us down long enough to dream. To imagine. To listen. It was not just warmth. It was wonder. Not just heat, but home.

Fire became the first gathering point. Before temples. Before governments. Before armies. It was the flame that said, "You are not alone." In many indigenous cultures, the fire circle still remains sacred. It is the center of ceremony, the source of stories, the heartbeat of the tribe. To build fire together is to say, "This is a place of presence. Of power. Of people becoming."

The Viking Funeral Pyre: Flame as Passage to Glory

The historical expression of fire that captured my attention most during this research was that of the Norwegian people known as Vikings. In Viking belief, death was not the end. It was the doorway to Valhalla, the great hall of the gods, where fallen warriors feast and fight forever. To reach it, the soul had to cross over, and fire was the ferry.

Imagine the rugged coastlines of Norway, cold mist curling across the fjords, pine trees bending beneath the weight of the northern wind. A longship rests on a stone beach, heavy with shields, blades, and furs. Upon it lies a warrior, his hands wrapped around the hilt of his sword, eyes closed, face weathered by war and time. Villagers gather with torches in hand, their voices low. They are not mourning a loss. They are preparing a passage.

The chieftain steps forward and sets the ship ablaze. Flames leap like wolves, racing up the sail. Heat pulses against the faces of those who watch. Sparks scatter into the darkening sky, rising toward the heavens like a soul ascending to glory. The fire becomes both honor and transformation. It consumes the mortal vessel, yet releases the spirit.

For the Norse, to burn was to rise. Not merely to be remembered, but to become legend. The Vikings understood fire as the ultimate act of release, not only destruction, but elevation. They did not bury their warriors. They entrusted them to the flame and believed they were set free.

"Cattle die, kinsmen die, all men are mortal. But the good name never dies of one who has done well."

– Hávamál, Norse Poetic Edda

Today, we may not sail burning ships, but the metaphor remains. Sometimes something must burn so that something eternal can begin. The Vikings burned their dead not only to honor them, but to release them into something greater. In many ways, the same is true in our spiritual and personal lives. There are moments when we find ourselves standing on the shore of something unknown, clutching what feels familiar: our safety, our plans, our reputation, our comfort zones.

And God whispers:
"Set it on fire."

Not to destroy you, but to **release you**. To awaken something new.

Letting go in fire means we stop clinging to what once served us but no longer carries us. It means trusting that what feels like an ending may actually be the beginning of a life marked by deeper purpose, greater courage, and unshakable clarity. Sometimes it is burning the plan you had so you can walk into the calling God has prepared. Sometimes it is surrendering the version of yourself that plays it safe so the wild, obedient, and bold version of you can rise. Sometimes it is releasing a title, a fear, or a timeline, because fire does not wait for your comfort to catch up with your calling.

Like the Viking ship, your faith journey may require you to light the match, let it go, watch it burn, and believe that something sacred will rise from the flame.

The Dance of Flame and the Human Heart

Fire does something to us, not only practically, but spiritually. Sit in front of a flame and you will notice your breath deepens, your mind quiets, and your soul begins to listen. It draws out what you have buried. It reveals what you have forgotten. It becomes a holy invitation. Even before Scripture speaks, creation testifies. Fire refines, purifies, and transforms. It is both tender and terrifying. And so, too, is the work of God in the soul. Not always soft. Not always safe. But always purposeful.

Nature shows us that after fire, the earth breathes again. New shoots break through ash. Some trees, like the jack pine, hold their seeds in tight cones that will not open without flame. It is as if God wired creation to respond to fire with rebirth. So why would our souls be any different?

God uses fire to:

Burn away what no longer serves us. The old habits, false identities, and misplaced affections.

Illuminate what is true. Our purpose, our calling, our identity as His sons and daughters.

Prepare the soil of our hearts for something deeper, something lasting, something eternal.

These spiritual fires may come in unexpected ways. It may be through a crisis that strips away illusion and forces you to see clearly, or a betrayal that teaches you to trust God more than people, or perhaps a transition that leaves you disoriented but desperate for God's presence. It might come through a calling that will not leave you alone, no matter how long you run. In these moments, you stand in the flame. It is hot. It is humbling. But it is holy. Because God does not waste fire. He wields it.

Think of Moses and the burning bush. A shepherd doing routine work, suddenly interrupted by fire that did not consume. God was speaking. And that fire would call him into deliverance, into destiny. Think of Isaiah, undone by the holiness of God. A coal taken from the altar touched his lips. It cleansed him. It commissioned him. Think of the disciples on the road to Emmaus, saying, "Did not our hearts burn within us?" (Luke 24:32). Jesus had been walking with them, and the Word was setting something aflame in their souls.

This is what happens when the fire of God meets the human heart:

- Comfort is traded for calling.
- Routine is exchanged for revelation.
- Fear is burned away by holy boldness.

But here is the paradox. Most of us want resurrection without fire. We want revival without refining. We want destiny without the discomfort that births it. Yet fire, in the hands of God, is never for our destruction. It is for our distinction. It marks us. It refines us. It sends us.

So if you are walking through heat right now, do not despise it. Ask, "Lord, what are You burning away? What are You preparing me for?" Let your fire become fuel. Let it become focus. Let it become faith. Because what burns in you today may be the light that leads someone else tomorrow.

Blowing on the Ember: Rekindling Wild Faith

Sometimes even the brightest faith can seem to burn low, reduced to a glowing ember hidden beneath the ashes of disappointment, exhaustion, or doubt. Yet anyone who has tended a campfire knows that if you gently blow on an ember, oxygen rushes in and the ember glows brighter, often reigniting into flame.

Spiritually, our hearts work the same way.

God is a master at rekindling faith that feels almost gone. If you find yourself weary, discouraged, or spiritually cold, you must find ways to blow on the ember and invite God to bring your fire back to life.

On the television show *Dual Survival*, two survival experts are often stranded in rain-soaked, muddy environments where finding a spark of fire can seem impossible. Yet no matter how wet the world around them becomes, they know fire is essential. It brings warmth, hope, safety, and even the possibility of rescue.

When everything is wet, here is what they do:

- **Dig for Dryness:** They peel back soggy outer bark, split logs, or dig into rotting stumps to uncover dry shavings or resin-rich fatwood hidden inside. Even when everything appears soaked, they search for the dry core within.
- **Make Feather Sticks:** Using a knife, they carefully carve thin curls from the driest wood, creating more surface area. These tiny feathers can catch a spark even when larger logs cannot.
- **Strike Again and Again:** With patience, they continue striking a ferro rod or flint, knowing persistence is essential. Sometimes

they use steel wool and a battery, a glass lens and sunlight, or whatever is available to coax an ember to life.

- **Shelter and Nurture:** They shield the smallest ember from wind and rain, blowing gently and feeding it with the tiniest dry twigs and leaves before adding anything larger.

Even in the wettest, most discouraging circumstances, the potential for fire remains. It simply requires extra effort, creative thinking, and a refusal to quit. Start small. Protect the ember. Keep nurturing it. Fire can return, even in the harshest places.

When your faith feels soaked by disappointment or difficulty, remember the lesson. Dig deep. Start small. Do not give up. God can bring your ember back to life, even in the rain.

Reflecting the Glory of God

God Almighty is raising up a generation, not one that performs for applause, but one that reflects His glory. He is not after showmanship. He is after purity. He is looking for vessels made in His image and marked by His character. In Malachi 3:1–3, we see the prophetic image of a coming Refiner. This Refiner is not a distant force. He is personal. He comes to His temple, and He comes with fire, not to destroy, but to purify. The sons of Levi, representing the priesthood, were set apart to minister to God. Today, we, the Church, are that priesthood. As 1 Peter 2:9 ***declares, we are a chosen generation, a royal priesthood, called to proclaim the praises of the One who brought us out of darkness and into His marvelous light***. But before proclamation comes purification. God does not call us to shine without first refining us.

In a great house, Paul wrote to Timothy, there are many vessels, some of gold and silver, and others of wood and clay. Some are used for honor, and some for dishonor. The difference is purity. Second Timothy 2:21 ***urges us to cleanse ourselves so that we may be sanctified and ready for the Master's use***. The Greek word for ***honorable*** is ***timē***, meaning precious. The word for ***dishonorable*** is ***atimia***, meaning shameful, base, or vile. God calls us to be vessels of honor, and that requires purging, a separating of the precious from the vile. Jeremiah 15:19 says, ***"If you***

extract the precious from the vile, you shall be as My mouth." What a powerful image: speaking for God, shaped by the fires that purified us.

This refining is not for the unbeliever. It is for the believer. God purifies those who already belong to Him. Why? So we can reveal His nature to a world stuck in darkness. The process is personal, painful, and holy. Just like natural gold, our hearts must go through refining fire to become what we were meant to be.

Gold, in its natural state, is rarely pure. It is mixed with other elements such as copper, iron, and nickel that harden it and dull its beauty. These foreign elements are called alloys. The more alloy present, the harder and more corrupted the gold becomes. The less alloy, the purer, softer, and more pliable it becomes. In the same way, a pure heart is soft, teachable, and moldable in the hands of God.

Scripture warns us in Hebrews 3:7–13 not to harden our hearts. The heart, when mixed with sin and pride, becomes resistant and unable to hear God's voice clearly. This is the tragedy of much of the modern Church. We may look good outwardly, but inside we have allowed alloy, bitterness, selfishness, and compromise to take root. We have a form of godliness but lack power because our hearts are no longer tender before the Lord. We have traded love for others for self-love. We chase comfort over calling. We want the benefits of the Kingdom without surrendering to the King. Yet James 1:27 reminds us what pure religion looks like: ***caring for the vulnerable and keeping ourselves unspotted by the world.***

Gold has another quality. It resists corrosion. Unlike other metals that tarnish with time and exposure, true gold remains untarnished. Brass may resemble gold at first glance, but it quickly reveals its corruption. It shines on the outside yet lacks endurance. It is a counterfeit, a cheap substitute. This is why God allows testing. The testing reveals what is genuine and what is merely religious polish.

The refining of gold requires intense heat. The gold is placed into a crucible along with a powder called flux. Together they are placed into the furnace. As the heat rises, the gold melts and the impurities, called dross, rise to the surface. The refiner carefully watches the process, never leaving the crucible, and uses a ladle to skim away the impurities. What remains is pure gold.

God uses this same process in our lives. Isaiah 1:25–26 describes it clearly: ***"I will thoroughly purge away your dross… and afterward you shall be called the city of righteousness."*** The fire is not for punishment. It is for purification.

Trials and tribulations are the furnace in which God refines us. First Peter 1:6–7 calls our faith more precious than gold and says it is tested by fire so that it may result in praise, honor, and glory at the revealing of Jesus Christ. I do not believe God causes every trial, but I do believe He allows them. He uses them. He meets us in the fire, and He transforms us through it. Isaiah 48:10 says, ***"I have refined you, but not as silver; I have tested you in the furnace of affliction."*** God does not share His glory with another. He will not allow a proud heart to rob Him of the work only He can accomplish.

And here is the truth: we cannot see our own impurities without the fire. You cannot see what is in the gold until the heat draws it out. Likewise, you cannot see what is in your heart until you are placed in the heat of life. When the dross rises, when sin, pride, jealousy, unforgiveness, and fear surface, we are given a choice. Will we repent and allow the Refiner to remove it? Or will we blame others and prolong our time in the wilderness? God does not cleanse us against our will. Second Timothy 2:21 says we must cleanse ourselves. This is a divine partnership.

But the reward of a pure heart is immeasurable. Matthew 5:8 declares, ***"Blessed are the pure in heart, for they shall see God."*** To see Him, not only hear about Him, not only sing to Him, but truly see Him. Psalm 19:12 records David's prayer: ***"Cleanse me from secret faults." Even the hidden things, Lord, purify them***. Proverbs 25:4–5 gives a beautiful image of purpose restored: ***"Remove the dross from the silver, and the silversmith can produce a vessel. Take away the wicked from before the king, and his throne is established in righteousness."***

God wants to produce something holy, useful, and radiant in your life. But first comes the fire. Then the skimming. And then the glory.

The Match and the Striker: The Power of Potential

Faith on fire is like a single wooden match resting in your hand. On its own, a match is full of potential, yet it has not fulfilled its purpose. It is only when the match is struck, when willingness meets risk, that everything changes. The moment the match meets the striker, friction produces a spark, and what was once dormant becomes dynamic. In an instant, light and heat burst forth, and the match is transformed.

In your spiritual journey, you are the match. God's invitation, His nudge, is the striker. When you respond in obedience, even with trembling hands, the conditions are set for something powerful to happen. Your yes, no matter how uncertain or small, meets God's faithfulness and ignites a spark of faith that can illuminate your world and the lives of those around you.

A lit match may seem insignificant, yet it can start a campfire, brighten a dark room, or ignite a wildfire. The same is true of your obedience. It may feel small, but once your faith is set ablaze, it carries the potential to bring warmth, light, and transformation to places you never imagined.

The miracle is not only that the match lights. It is what happens when the flame spreads. Your leap of faith can inspire others, awaken revival within your family, and become a catalyst for God's work in your community. The fire does not remain contained within you. It grows. It moves. It multiplies.

The Prairie Fire Effect

In the heartland of America, prairie fires are both feared and respected. Unlike a small campfire or a controlled burn, a true prairie fire can sweep across the landscape with remarkable speed and power, igniting everything in its path. What begins as a single spark, perhaps a lightning strike, a tossed match, or a patch of dry grass heated by the sun, can quickly become an unstoppable force that transforms the entire ecosystem.

What allows a prairie fire to spread so rapidly?

- **Unseen Connections:** Tall grasses, roots, and dry brush interweave beneath the surface. Once ignited, the fire leaps from blade to blade, fueled by wind and ready conditions. Nothing remains isolated for long.
- **Wind as Fuel:** Wind drives the fire forward, sometimes in unexpected directions. A steady breeze can turn a small blaze into a sweeping wildfire.
- **No Turning Back:** Once a prairie fire gains momentum, it becomes nearly impossible to contain. Heat, light, and energy consume what lies in its path, leaving behind scorched earth, yet also preparing the ground for new growth.

What does this mean for your faith?

A single life set on fire by God can do far more than bring warmth to a personal circle. Like a prairie fire, wild faith is contagious. When you live with boldness and take risks for God, your passion and courage cross boundaries of family, church, community, and culture. Others catch the flame through your example. Your story, your prayers, and your obedience become like wind, carrying the fire further than you could ever predict.

Just as the prairie is never the same after the fire, a community touched by genuine wild faith is permanently changed, often in ways only God can see at first. The old is cleared away, and fresh growth becomes possible.

Coaching Insight

The Big Truth

God does not ignite faith to impress others. He ignites it to transform you. Fire is not punishment. It is preparation. What God allows to burn away is never greater than what He intends to reveal.

The Mirror Question

What has God been allowing to heat up in your life that you have been trying to escape instead of surrender to? What might He be refining rather than removing?

The Thirty First Footstep

Name one area where resistance has risen as pressure increased. Instead of asking God to take the fire away, choose to ask what He may be shaping in you through it. Identify one act of obedience that aligns with refinement rather than avoidance.

The Inner Work

Refining fire often reveals what was hidden long before it became harmful. Pride, fear, control, and distraction surface when heat is applied. This exposure is not condemnation. It is invitation. God does not shame what He refines. He stays close to it. The fire does not mean God has stepped back. It often means He is nearer than ever.

Reflection Prompt

What emotions surface when you consider God using fire to shape you? Where do you sense tenderness or resistance when you imagine letting go of what no longer belongs?

Prayer of Alignment

God, I trust You as Refiner and Redeemer. I release what You are burning away and receive what You are forming within me. Purify my heart, soften my spirit, and ignite my faith for Your purposes. Let my life reflect Your glory, not my comfort. I choose surrender over control and trust You in the fire. Amen.

CHAPTER 6: IMPOSSIBLE INVITATIONS

When God Dares You to Dream Beyond Logic

"God is looking for people through whom He can do the impossible. What a pity we plan only things we can do by ourselves."

— A.W. Tozer

There are moments in the life of faith when God disrupts everything familiar with a single, unshakable call: Come. It does not always arrive with thunder or visions. Sometimes it begins as a whisper, a stirring, a relentless ache in your spirit that refuses to be silenced. It may surface in the stillness of prayer, in the chaos of transition, or through an unexpected opportunity that seems too large for your ability and too wild for your timeline.

God does not call us into what is comfortable. He calls us into what seems impossible, into territory that defies logic and exceeds our résumés. He invites us to dream not according to what we can manage, but according to what He can accomplish. He calls us to trust Him beyond the boundaries of our reason, beyond what our families expect, and even beyond what we believe we are capable of. Why? Because he is not interested in safe obedience. He is after surrendered hearts.

Think about the stories that shape our faith. God told Abraham, a childless old man, that he would become the father of nations. He told Noah to build a massive boat on dry land when no rain had fallen. He called Moses, an exile who struggled with speech, to confront Pharaoh and lead a nation. Each invitation carried the same theme. It sounded ridiculous. Illogical. Impossible. Yet every one of those calls was soaked in divine purpose.

God specializes in impossible invitations. He does not ask us to understand everything. He asks us to trust Him. He does not wait for us to feel ready. He asks us to follow anyway. These moments are not designed to inflate our ego. They are meant to strip us of self-reliance and lead us into dependence on Him. It is in the impossible that God receives the greatest glory, because it is where our strength runs out, and His begins.

Maybe you have experienced this tension. You feel a pull in your spirit to begin something that does not make sense. To give generously when your budget is tight. To forgive when the pain still lingers. To lead when you feel unqualified. To write, move, speak, build, adopt, or believe in something far beyond what you could orchestrate on your own.

You question whether it is really God or just your imagination. Yet deep down you know. It is Him. The thought will not leave you. The invitation keeps returning.

That is the beginning of a holy invitation.

It rarely arrives with certainty or strategy. More often, it appears as tension between faith and fear, calling and comfort, courage and caution. And within that tension, God asks one simple question: Will you trust Me?

The truth is that God's impossible invitations are less about the dream and more about your dependency. He is not trying to see how much you can accomplish. He is inviting you to walk with Him without knowing the entire path. When you step into the impossible with God, you discover that He Himself is the provision, the strength, the strategy, and the outcome.

If your life feels too tidy, too predictable, too contained, perhaps you are standing at the edge of your own impossible invitation. And perhaps it is time to say yes.

"Perseverance and spirit have done wonders in all ages."
— George Washington

The Birth of a Nation: Faith Beneath Fire

In the bitter chill of December 1776, the American colonies stood on the edge of collapse. The dream of independence, once shouted in town halls and written boldly on parchment, was nearly extinguished beneath the crushing advance of British forces. Defeat after defeat had left George Washington's Continental Army ragged, outnumbered, and half-starved. They had no grand capital, no seasoned army, and no guaranteed aid. Many soldiers had no shoes, leaving bloody footprints in the snow. By every military measure, it was an impossible moment.

Yet that was when Washington made one of the boldest decisions in American history.

On the night of December 25, while much of the world celebrated Christmas in warmth and comfort, Washington gathered his troops along the frozen banks of the Delaware River. The mission was simple in description and terrifying in reality. They would cross the icy, dangerous waters under the cover of darkness and launch a surprise attack against Hessian forces in Trenton, New Jersey.

The men moved quietly through the night. Ice cracked beneath the boats. Snow and wind cut through the darkness. Many were sick. Some would not survive the journey. Still, they pressed forward. They did not move because they were strong. They moved because they believed. They believed liberty was worth the risk. They believed tyranny would not have the final word. They believed that something unseen, a future not yet realized, was calling them forward.

When the attack came, they succeeded.

The victory at Trenton was more than a military triumph. It became a spark. A flame that proved the revolution was not over. It showed that courage, faith, and daring could change the direction of history.

This was not a war fought by perfect men. These were farmers, printers, teachers, and pastors, many of whom had never held a musket before. Yet they fought with conviction. They carried a vision of a nation where freedom would not belong only to the powerful, but would be recognized as a God-given right.

Centuries later, it is easy to read these events as if they were inevitable. In reality, nothing about that moment was certain. Everything appeared stacked against them. Logic pointed toward surrender. The world insisted it could not be done. Yet they moved forward anyway.

They were fueled by a vision of what could be. They gave birth to a nation not by strength alone, but by a form of wild faith. Faith in God. Faith in freedom. Faith in one another. Faith in a future that had never yet been seen.

Marked by Mission: When a Thumbprint Becomes a Testimony

Early in 2000, I was a student at Central Bible College in Springfield, Missouri. One of my favorite parts of those years was not only the theology classes or ministry training. It was the student-led chapel services woven between our classes and the rush toward lunch. Each day we gathered, hungry for God and spiritually expectant. One particular service has remained with me ever since.

That day, Steve Saint, the son of the late missionary Nate Saint, was the guest speaker. He did not come with hype or polish. He came with a legacy. He shared a story filled with faith, sacrifice, and the impossible love of God. As he spoke, it felt as though the walls of that chapel faded and the jungles of Ecuador stood before us.

He spoke about Operation Auca, a mission that began with fire in the hearts of five young men, including his father, Nate, and a friend named Jim Elliot. These men were not thrill seekers or reckless adventurers. They understood the risks clearly. The Huaorani people, who were then called the Auca, a Quechua word meaning savage, were known for violence and deep isolation. No outsider had ever contacted them and survived. Yet the call of the Gospel burned too strongly to ignore.

Nate Saint served as a missionary pilot with Mission Aviation Fellowship. Using his small yellow Piper aircraft, he flew over Huaorani territory again and again. With each flight, the team developed a plan to communicate peace and build trust from the air. They created a method using a circling flight pattern and lowered gifts to the tribe with a bucket tied to a rope. With every flight, they sent tools, food, and small tokens of goodwill. Over time, something remarkable happened. The Huaorani began leaving gifts in the bucket for the missionaries as well.

Eventually, the men believed enough trust had been established to attempt face-to-face contact. They selected a sandy riverbank deep in the jungle as their landing place. They called it Palm Beach. On January 3, 1956, Nate Saint, Jim Elliot, Ed McCully, Roger Youderian, and Pete Fleming landed there and set up camp.

For several days, the men waited and prayed. They made contact with a few members of the tribe, exchanged gifts, and believed the relationship was beginning to grow. But on January 8, tragedy struck. All five men were speared to death by a group of Huaorani warriors who responded out of fear and suspicion rather than trust. The news of their deaths shocked the world. Yet what the world saw as failure, God was already shaping into redemption.

Steve Saint shared how those events forever marked his life. Not only through the loss of his father, but through what followed. The widows of the slain missionaries, including Elisabeth Elliot and Nate's sister Rachel Saint, did something that stunned the world. They returned to the jungle. Not for revenge. Not even for justice. They returned with forgiveness.

Over time, something miraculous unfolded. The very people who had killed those five missionaries came to faith in Jesus Christ. Entire families were baptized in the same river where the blood of those men had once flowed. The tribe was transformed, not through force or control, but through love, perseverance, and wild faith.

Years later, Steve Saint developed deep friendships with the very men who had taken his father's life. One of them was Mincaye, who later became like a grandfather to Steve's children and traveled with him to share their story around the world.

As Steve spoke in the chapel that day, there was no resentment in his voice. There was peace. There was a purpose. There was a clear sense that when we say yes to God, even at great cost, He writes stories far beyond our understanding. I remember sitting there gripped by the holy tension of it all. Death and resurrection. Fear and faith. Grief and grace.

It was not simply a missionary story. It was an invitation to live a life where nothing is held back. Not even our safety. Not even our future. Operation Auca did not end in tragedy. It began in sacrifice and finished in redemption.

After the chapel service ended, a small group gathered near the front of the room. I walked forward, my heart still stirred by what I had heard. There stood Steve Saint beside a man whose presence carried a quiet weight beyond words. Mincaye. The very man who had once been among those who killed Steve's father now stood beside him like family. I reached out and shook their hands.

Steve's handshake was strong and steady, the grip of a man who had long been anchored in purpose. Mincaye's grip was firm yet gentle. His hands were weathered, shaped by the hard life of the jungle, yet redeemed by grace. Then something unforgettable happened.

Mincaye pulled out a small red stamp pad, the kind missionaries sometimes use when language barriers make written signatures difficult. Without ceremony, he pressed his thumb into the ink and gently placed the imprint on the inside cover of my Bible. A red thumbprint.

A mark once associated with bloodshed, now transformed into a seal of peace. That print was more than ink. It was a legacy. It was forgiveness made visible. It was the Gospel, not as a concept, but as a living story. A red thumbprint pressed into the pages of my Bible.

Even now, when I think about that Bible and that red thumbprint, I remember the story behind it. I remember that faith is not always logical. Sometimes it is impossible. Sometimes it is messy, dangerous, and costly. But it is always worth it.

"He is no fool, who gives what he cannot keep, to gain what he cannot lose."

— Jim Elliot

When the Invitation Feels Too Big for You

When we sense a call to something greater, whether it is a leadership opportunity, a creative dream, a step toward purpose, or a challenge that stretches us beyond comfort, our first reaction is often not excitement but resistance. Something inside tightens. Our inner critic awakens. We begin rehearsing all the reasons we are not ready, not qualified, and not enough.

It is important to name this experience for what it truly is. It is the natural tension between calling and capacity, between invitation and identity. This is the place where many people turn back, mistaking discomfort for disqualification. Yet greatness rarely begins with confidence. It begins with a yes spoken in the middle of trembling.

Psychologically, this moment often triggers what is known as imposter syndrome. It is the internal narrative that whispers, "You are a fraud," "You are only pretending," or "If people really knew you, they would not believe in you." Even high achievers experience this, especially when stepping into roles that feel larger than their history or credentials.

Spiritually, however, these moments are often invitations to co-labor with God rather than perform for Him. He is not calling you because you are flawless. He is calling you because you are willing. When you feel least ready, you are often most dependent. That dependence becomes the soil where faith grows wild, and roots reach deep.

Instead of rushing to escape the discomfort, one of the most powerful practices is to sit with the invitation itself. Ask honest questions. Why is this stirring something in me? Is this simply fear, or is it reverence for what could be possible?

Bring your whole heart into conversation with God. This is not about hyping yourself up or forcing doubt to disappear. It is about sifting through your emotions until the truth rises to the surface. In that place, prayer becomes less about asking for signs and more about surrendering to a process. You may find yourself praying, "God, if this is from You, prepare me. Change me. Give me the courage to respond."

You may not hear a booming voice. More often, clarity arrives through stillness, confirmation, and quiet alignment.

You do not have to discern this alone. Community matters deeply. When you share what you are sensing with a trusted mentor, coach, or spiritually mature friend, they can help you see beyond your own blind spots. Their questions may uncover what you already know deep within you. This invitation is speaking to your core identity, not your current résumé. And that is the point.

You are not stepping into something you have already mastered. You are stepping into something you were created to grow into.

The path forward does not require a master plan. It requires a first step. Do not wait for the entire staircase to appear before you step off the landing. Invitations to greatness rarely arrive with ease or full clarity. But they often come with an inner resonance. A pull. A restlessness. A whisper that says, This might be the way forward.

That whisper is holy ground. Do not wait until you feel fearless. Walk forward while you still feel unsure. Wild faith is not the absence of fear. It is obedience in the presence of it. What if the very thing that feels impossible is the exact place where God intends to show that with Him, all things are possible?

One of the most liberating spiritual truths is this. Your identity is not tied to your success. Your worth is not measured by how flawless your obedience becomes. You are not what you accomplish. You are who God calls you to be. Beloved. Chosen. Purposed.

Let God anchor your identity deeply before you chase results. When you do, your steps will no longer be driven by performance but by purpose. You will move forward not from pressure but from peace.

In that stillness, you begin to discern the source of the invitation. Ask yourself honest questions. Is this call driven by ego, or inspired by God? Does it create anxious striving, or does it awaken a holy ache that refuses to disappear?

God's invitations do not always come with comfort, but they do come with clarity. There is an inner resonance that continues to return. Once you recognize it, make space to pray and prepare. Journal your thoughts. Take time to walk. Fast if needed. Sit in silence. Ask God, "What is the first step You want me to take?"

Often, you will not receive a full map. You will receive the next stone in the path. Then take that step. Make the call. Submit the application. Schedule the meeting. You do not have to know everything. You simply need to move forward in faith.

As you move, surround yourself with reminders of truth. Fill your life with Scripture, worship, and people who speak life into your journey. Write declarations and keep them near you. Words such as "God equips those He calls," or "My weakness is the place where His strength appears." Return to those truths whenever doubt clouds your confidence.

Above all, remember that resistance is not always a warning sign. Sometimes it is confirmation. The enemy rarely attacks what poses no threat.

When obstacles appear, when your confidence shakes, and discouragement begins to whisper, do not retreat. Anchor deeper. Greatness rarely grows in easy soil. Yet it flourishes when you refuse to abandon the seed God has planted within you.

Walking with Purpose: Living with Intentionality

Being intentional is not simply about having goals or routines. It is about aligning your inner compass with what matters most. It is the quiet resolve to stop living on autopilot. It is choosing to say yes with clarity rather than out of guilt, and refusing to drift aimlessly through seasons without anchoring to purpose. Walking with purpose begins in the soul, where clarity is born not from hustle, but from holy surrender.

When you live with intention, you no longer allow your schedule to be dictated by urgency alone. You begin to ask deeper questions. Is this assignment aligned with my calling? Does this relationship feed or drain the flame God has placed within me? Am I moving out of pressure or out of peace?

Intentionality teaches you to pause before reacting. It forms the habit of responding with wisdom. Over time, it reshapes your time, your energy, your prayers, and even your conversations.

Spiritually, intentional living means you are not waiting to stumble into purpose. You are partnering with God to step into it each day. It means opening the Word not as a checklist, but as a lifeline. It means establishing spiritual rhythms. Not rigid routines, but life-giving disciplines that create space for grace, reflection, and communion with the Lord.

You begin to build margin for the sacred instead of squeezing God into what is left over. When you are intentional, even your no becomes an act of faith. You stop trying to be everything to everyone and begin focusing on being faithful to the One who called you.

As you live this way, you start noticing what truly matters. Divine interruptions. Sacred assignments disguised as ordinary moments. The still small voice is inviting you to slow down and listen.

Walking with purpose does not always mean you know the entire map. But it does mean you trust the One who guides your steps. Intentionality becomes the bridge between hearing God and obeying Him. It is the daily decision not simply to believe in God, but to walk with Him. Slowly. Honestly. Boldly.

Because in the end, your impact will not be measured by how busy you were, but by how present you were to the voice of God and how faithfully you followed it.

A powerful example of intentional living in my own life is the way my wife and I began our journey as house parents at an all-girls group home in Tahlequah, Oklahoma. The home was part of Circle of Care, a Methodist-run ministry focused on providing stability, healing, and hope to young girls from broken and often painful backgrounds.

It became a season of quiet formation for us. We were not simply managing a household. We were stepping into the stories of girls who had seen too much too soon. We helped with homework, dried tears after therapy sessions, mediated roommate conflicts, and prayed silently as we tucked them into bed each night.

It was a crash course in compassion, patience, and spiritual resilience. We learned to listen more than we spoke and to lead from gentleness rather than control. The Holy Spirit did some of His most powerful work not in chapel services, but during late-night conversations at the kitchen table or whispered prayers behind closed doors.

Little did we know, this was only the beginning.

God began stirring our hearts again. Not away from ministry, but deeper into it. We were invited to serve at CompACT Family Services, a faith-based Assemblies of God group home in Hot Springs, Arkansas. This time, we would serve as house parents for high school boys.

The transition was more than geographic. It was spiritual. What awaited us there was a new level of challenge and calling.

These were not just boys. They were sons without stable fathers, warriors without armor, young men hardened by the world yet deeply hungry for purpose. Some had moved from foster home to foster home. Others had already encountered the justice system. Many were angry. Most were hurting.

But God was writing a story, and He invited us to be part of it.

Life at CompACT was not easy. Some nights were filled with shouting, and some days ended in tears. We dealt with broken curfews, vandalized furniture, and more than a few heartbreaking disclosures. Yet alongside the chaos, something sacred was unfolding.

Slowly, trust began to grow. Respect started to form. We watched hard exteriors soften under consistent love and correction. We prayed over their rooms, led devotional moments during chores, and spent countless hours simply listening to their stories. Stories that broke our hearts and stretched our faith.

Intentionality became our lifeline. Every word mattered. Every boundary mattered. Every "I am proud of you" carried the weight of eternity. We were not simply managing behavior. We were partnering with God to rewrite identities.

Looking back, we did not always feel ready. We certainly did not have all the answers. But we shared one simple thing. A yes to God.

That yes shaped not only the young men living under our roof, but also our marriage, our calling, and our understanding of ministry itself.

Today, we have the privilege of being spiritual grandparents to another generation of our girls and boys from those unforgettable seasons in the group homes. Some now have families of their own. Others still call or write when life grows heavy.

Each connection reminds us that intentional love leaves a lasting legacy. We did not simply plant seeds. We are now witnessing fruit. And we are still watching it grow.

A Personal Invitation to Step Out with Wild Faith

Friend, you do not need to have everything figured out to walk with purpose. My wife and I did not. We simply made ourselves available, and God met us in that willingness.

Maybe your calling does not look like a group home. But there is a space in this world that only your obedience can fill. There is a child, a neighbor, a ministry, or a dream waiting for your yes.

Wild faith does not wait for comfort. It moves when the whisper comes.

This is your invitation. Not to chase perfection, but to show up. To take the next faithful step. To believe that what you carry, no matter how small it feels, becomes sacred when placed in God's hands.

The same God who met us in the middle of chaos and calling will meet you, too.

So let me ask you:

What step is stirring inside you?

Where is God nudging you to live with wild faith and intentional love?

Say yes.

Even if your hands tremble.

Even if you do not know what lies on the other side.

You do not have to see one hundred feet ahead.

Just trust Him with the next thirty-one.

Coaching Insight

The Big Truth

God's impossible invitations are not tests of your ability. They are invitations into deeper trust. When God calls you beyond logic, He is not asking you to prove yourself. He is asking you to walk with Him.

The Mirror Question

What invitation has been stirring in you that feels larger than your confidence or clarity? Where have you been waiting to feel ready instead of choosing to trust?

The Thirty-First Footstep

Name the invitation you have been resisting because it feels impossible. Identify one small obedient response that moves you toward trust rather than certainty. Faith rarely begins with the full picture. It begins with the next step.

The Inner Work

Impossible invitations often surface fear, self-doubt, and questions about worth. These reactions do not disqualify you. They reveal the places where dependency on God must deepen. God does not call you because you are complete. He calls you because He is. When you stop measuring yourself by readiness and start anchoring yourself in identity, courage begins to rise.

Reflection Prompt

What emotions surface when you imagine saying yes to this invitation?
What would trusting God look like if you released the need to control the outcome?

Prayer of Alignment

God, I bring You my hesitation, my questions, and my fear. I release the need to understand everything before I move. I choose trust over logic and obedience over comfort. Strengthen my faith as I respond to Your invitation and lead me one step at a time. Amen.

Chapter 7:
Prayers That Shake Heaven

Trading Safe Requests for Mountain-Moving Intercession

"I am not moved by what I see. I am not moved by what I feel. I am moved only by what I believe."
— Smith Wigglesworth

Wild Faith That Shakes Heaven

Wild faith does not live only in belief. It lives in partnership. It shows up when prayer and obedience move together. Heaven shaking prayer is rarely passive. It is active trust. It is the kind of prayer that dares to ask and then dares to act as though God has heard.

If you pray for rain, you grab an umbrella. If you ask for open doors, you begin walking toward them.

Prayer that shakes heaven is not about saying the right words. It is about aligning your life with what you are asking God to do. That is where faith becomes visible. That is where prayer gains weight.

Many people pray cautiously because they fear disappointment. They soften their requests. They generalize their needs. They stay vague in case God does not move. But wild faith prays with clarity. It names the need. It speaks the diagnosis. It calls the prodigal by name. It writes the number down. It does not hide behind spiritual politeness. Specific prayers create unmistakable testimonies. Yet prayer is not the finish line. It is the ignition point.

Wild faith puts feet to prayer. It applies for the job before confidence arrives. It makes the phone call before courage feels steady. It schedules the appointment. It tests the movement. It forgives before the apology comes.

Faith often feels risky because it requires movement before certainty. That is not recklessness. That is trust.

One simple practice that has strengthened this partnership in my life is keeping what I call a Wild Faith Journal. Write the prayer. Write the Scripture. Write the step you feel prompted to take. Write the date. When God answers, record that too. Testimonies become anchors when faith feels thin. They remind you that God has moved before and He can move again. I learned this practice in an unexpected way.

The Napkin That Carries a Yes

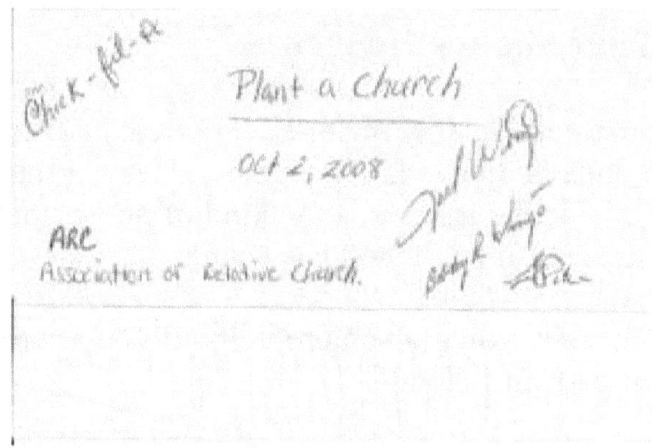

It wasn't a journal. It wasn't planned. It wasn't even neat. It was a napkin.

I remember the moment clearly. I was sitting in an ordinary place, but facing a decision that felt anything but ordinary. Something inside me knew this wasn't just another thought passing through. This was a line in the sand moment.

I didn't have clarity. I didn't have a timeline. I didn't have guarantees.

But I had a stirring in my spirit. I knew if I didn't capture it right then, fear would start negotiating with obedience. So I grabbed what I had in front of me.

A napkin. And I wrote.

Not a sermon, nor a strategy. It was just three words that represented a prayer and a surrendered decision.

"Plant a Church"

October 2, 2008.

That was it… Simple words but they carried the weight of a yes.

I folded the napkin and tucked it away. I didn't know what would come next. I didn't know how God would move. I only knew what He had met me in that moment.

Years passed

Life unfolded in ways that my wife and I could not have predicted. Some prayers were answered quickly. Others took time. Some doors opened wide. Others required endurance we didn't know we had.

And then one day, I found it again. That napkin.

The ink had faded but the moment was still alive. What struck me wasn't just what I had written. It was who I was when I wrote it.

Uncertain. Honest. Willing. What overwhelmed me even more was this:

God had been faithful to that yes and is still faithful as I write this book.

The napkin became more than a memory. It became witness. A reminder that heaven responds to surrendered moments, even when they are scribbled in haste and soaked in uncertainty.

When faith feels thin, those old words still speak. God was faithful then. He is faithful now.

Sometimes faith calls for symbolic action. In Scripture people walked, lifted, anointed, and stepped as expressions of trust. Today that may look like praying over a room, walking land you are believing for, or placing a name somewhere visible as a reminder that the prayer has not been forgotten.

These acts do not manipulate God. They align us with Him. Speak your prayers out loud. Declare Scripture with your own voice. Faith grows stronger when it is spoken, not only when it is thought.

Sometimes the wildest act of faith is moving before the door opens. Writing the first page. Buying the baby clothes. Starting the ministry. Celebrating provision before it arrives.

Wild faith believes God is faithful enough to meet you in motion.

Safe prayers maintain comfort.
Wild prayers invite transformation.

Safe prayers focus on survival.
Wild prayers focus on surrender.

Safe prayers ask for help getting through.
Wild prayers ask God to change what feels impossible.

Wild prayer is not louder.
It is braver.

Endurance That Shakes Heaven

Some of the most powerful prayers do not shake heaven immediately. Instead, they shape the one who prays.

Not every prayer is answered quickly. Not every silence means absence. Not every delay is denial. Sometimes God is doing a deeper work than simply changing circumstances. Sometimes He is forming a faith strong enough to carry what is coming next.

Scripture speaks honestly about this tension. Daniel prayed and fasted for weeks before breakthrough came, unaware that a spiritual battle was unfolding beyond what he could see. Jesus told the story of a widow who returned again and again, her persistence wearing down injustice not through force but through faithfulness. Even Jesus prayed in a garden where the answer did not remove the suffering but strengthened Him to endure it.

Endurance in prayer is not passive waiting. It is active trust. It is choosing to keep showing up when results are delayed. It is lifting your eyes toward heaven while your feet remain planted on hard ground. Enduring prayer does not beg God to care. It declares that He already does.

And that kind of faith, steady, persistent, and unrelenting, has a way of shaking heaven in its own time.

Endurance in prayer is not passive waiting. It is active trust.

There was a woman in our church whose story shaped my understanding of faith more than many dramatic miracles. Her name in this story is Helen. That is not her real name, but the story itself is true.

For many years, Helen prayed for her son Mark, who had wandered far from God. She also prayed faithfully for her husband. Time passed. Helen was faithful in our local church and always reminded everyone that God was going to bring salvation to her household. Through it all, she never stopped believing. She never stopped loving them. She never stopped praying.

The church family encouraged her, yet with disbelief that they would ever darken the doors. Still, she persisted to believe God.

And then it happened, Mark and his dad walked back into church. There was no spectacle. No announcement. Just grace.

Not long after, her husband also gave his heart to the Lord along with her son.

What had looked like silence for a long season had actually been shaping something deeper than Helen could see. Her prayers had not failed. They had been forming something.

Enduring prayer changes the one who intercedes. It stretches hope. It tempts numbness. It asks whether faith can survive without visible evidence.

Yet God honors prayers that refuse to quit. Not because they are loud, but because they are rooted in trust.

Some prayers take years because God is working on more than one heart at a time.

Faith That Holds When Nothing Changes

Wild faith is often associated with miracles and bold action. Yet sometimes the wildest faith is simply staying. It is showing up again. Praying again. Loving again. Enduring faith is a long obedience moving in the same direction.

I have walked with couples who remained committed when walking away seemed easier. There were years of tension. Years of prayer. Years spent learning how to listen again. Their miracle was not instant restoration, but gradual transformation. Today they mentor others, not because they were perfect, but because they endured.

Scripture honors this kind of faith. Abraham waited decades for the promise he had been given. Joseph endured pits and prisons before purpose unfolded. The woman with the issue of blood carried years of suffering before pressing through the crowd. Jesus Himself endured the cross, trusting the joy set before Him.

Endurance is not weakness. It is strength formed slowly over time. Sometimes wild faith looks like stubborn hope. Sometimes it looks like getting up in the morning when grief makes breathing difficult.

Sometimes it looks like continuing to serve when no one notices. These prayers matter. Heaven records them.

Enduring faith often looks like praying when you feel empty, loving when your heart aches, and showing up when results remain unseen. This is not faith that fades. This is faith that matures.

A Blessing Over the Weary Intercessor

- May you be strengthened in the waiting when answers feel delayed.
- May you be reminded that every prayer you have whispered in faith has been heard.
- May courage rise again in places where discouragement has tried to settle.
- May you sense God's nearness even when circumstances remain unchanged.
- May your endurance become a testimony that outlives the season of struggle.
- May you trust not only for outcomes, but for presence.
- And may you discover that the faith you thought was barely holding on has been holding heaven's attention all along.

Wild faith does not quit simply because time passes. It trusts because God remains faithful. Sometimes the prayers that shake heaven are the ones that refuse to stop echoing.

Faith in Practice

Enduring faith is not built in dramatic moments. It is shaped through repeated choices. This chapter invites you to pay attention to what you keep doing when nothing seems to change. Wild faith is not measured only by bold leaps forward. It is also revealed through the quiet discipline of remaining present, prayerful, and obedient over time.

As a Christian Life Coach, I often help people recognize the places where discouragement has quietly rewritten their expectations. When prayers appear unanswered, we tend to shrink our hope rather than strengthen our trust. This is where endurance becomes a spiritual practice.

Ask yourself where you have been tempted to quit internally even if you have not quit outwardly. Notice the areas where you continue to show up faithfully. Those places matter far more than you may realize.

One powerful step is to name what you are enduring and bring it honestly before God. Not with polished words, but with truth. Enduring faith grows when you stop pretending to be strong and instead choose to remain faithful. This is not about forcing optimism. It is about choosing alignment with God even when your emotions lag behind your obedience.

Another key practice is remembering. Return to the moments when God has been faithful in the past. Write those memories down. Speak them aloud. Let remembrance become fuel for the present. Endurance weakens when we forget, but it strengthens when we rehearse God's past faithfulness in the middle of current tension.

Finally, give yourself permission to define progress differently. Growth may look like softened reactions, deeper compassion, or the courage to pray again after silence. These are not small things. They are signs of a maturing faith.

Enduring faith does not rush the process. It trusts that God is working even when the work remains invisible. Wild faith is not always loud. Sometimes it is quiet, steady, and unseen. But it is never wasted.

Coaching Insight

The Big Truth

Enduring prayer is not a consolation prize. It is a form of spiritual strength. Some prayers do not shake heaven immediately, but they shape the one who prays. God is not absent in the waiting. He is forming a faith that can carry weight.

The Mirror Question

Where have you been tempted to quit internally even if you have not quit outwardly? What is your napkin moment? What have you quietly stopped asking God for because the wait has been long?

The Thirty First Footstep

Choose one prayer you have been carrying for a long time. Write it down in one clear sentence. Name the step. Mark the date. Pair it with one faithful action that aligns with it, even if nothing changes yet. Endurance grows when prayer and obedience remain connected.

The Inner Work

Waiting exposes what we believe about God's goodness, God's timing, and our own worth. Delay can stir discouragement, comparison, and the urge to protect ourselves from disappointment. This does not mean you lack faith. It means the deeper parts of your heart are being invited into trust.

Enduring faith is not passive resignation. It is active surrender. It continues showing up without demanding a timeline. It keeps loving without requiring immediate evidence. It keeps praying while choosing to believe that God is still working.

Reflection Prompt

What emotions surface when you imagine praying this same prayer again without an immediate answer?

Where do you feel the weight of waiting in your body, your thoughts, or your relationships?

Prayer of Alignment

Jesus, You see every prayer I have whispered and every tear that carried words I could not find. Strengthen me in the waiting. Guard my heart from discouragement and numbness. Teach me to trust You not only for outcomes, but for Your presence. Help me stay faithful, stay soft, and stay surrendered until Your answer comes in Your way and in Your time.

Amen.

CHAPTER 8:
INTO THE DEEP

Growing Wild Faith Beyond the Moment

"You cannot swim for new horizons until you have courage to lose sight of the shore."

-William Faulkner

There comes a moment in every journey of faith when the shoreline disappears.

It is the moment you step beyond the place where your feet can still touch. Beyond formulas and familiarity. Beyond the comfort of shallow waters. Up until now, your faith may have carried you through daily rhythms, quiet times, community groups, and Sunday services. But then something deeper begins to stir.

A call. Quiet, yet undeniable.
It does not shout. It beckons.
And it leads not toward certainty, but toward depth.
This is where wild faith begins to mature.

The deep is not chaotic. It is consecrated. It is the place where you are no longer supported by routine or sustained by the agreement of others. It is where the applause fades, the measurements lose meaning, and what remains is God and the trust it takes to keep following Him.

The deep is where God invites you to live beyond the moment. Beyond the initial yes. Beyond the emotional high of a mission trip, a conference, or a breakthrough. It is where He asks a quieter, weightier question.

Will you keep walking when the feeling fades? This is where wild faith moves from a spark to a steady flame. It is where you learn to remain, not because it is easy, but because He is present.

Some of us remain in shallow waters because they feel safe. Predictable. Measurable. But a life of deep faith was never meant to be evaluated by how composed it appears on the surface. It is shaped by how willing we are to move forward when the next step is not fully visible.

The deeper the water, the more you must trust what holds you. And what holds you is not darkness or danger. It is the everlasting arms of God.

When Peter stepped out of the boat, he had no map, only a voice. When Abraham packed his tent, he had no coordinates, only a promise. When you move into deeper waters, you lose sight of the bottom, but you gain clarity of the One who called you.

This chapter is an invitation to go there.

Not recklessly.
Not impulsively.
But intentionally.
Boldly.
Trustingly.

This is for those who are tired of standing ankle deep in a faith that only touches the surface. It is for those who are ready to go beneath, to wrestle, to wonder, to walk with God in places where comfort cannot follow.

Because in the deep, transformation is real.

Intimacy is raw.
The risk is great.
But so is the reward.

Several summers ago, my family, along with two other families, took a much needed vacation to Gulf Shores, Alabama. It was one of those trips you look back on with sand still in your shoes and stories still echoing in your mind.

One particular story came from the day the men separated from the rest of the group to take on what we were told would be an unforgettable offshore fishing adventure.

We chartered a boat, rose early, and set out before the sun. The sky was painted in soft pastels, and the sea seemed calm and inviting, at least at first. I am not a fisherman by nature, nor am I particularly drawn to open water. But there was something about that morning that felt bold, adventurous, and maybe even a little spiritual. And then the boat started rocking.

By the time we reached deep water, miles from shore, everything had changed. I was no longer captivated by the sunrise or casting a line over the rail. I was inside the cabin, flat on my back, praying for land.

That day taught me two things. First, never get on a deep sea vessel without motion sickness medication. Second, you do not catch big fish in the shallows.

The open sea, though unpredictable and uncomfortable, is where the real catch is found. That second lesson has stayed with me. It continues to speak, not just as a memory, but as a spiritual truth.

It reminds me of the prophetic vision in Ezekiel 47, where the prophet is led out from the temple into rising waters. First ankle deep. Then knee deep. Then waist deep. And finally, a river too deep to cross, water deep enough to swim in. It is a powerful picture of spiritual progression.

God does not intend for us to remain in shallow water. He invites us forward, step by step, into deeper trust, deeper surrender, and deeper faith.

Shallow water feels manageable. It offers control. It allows you to stand comfortably, to measure your footing, to maintain stability.

But the deep removes all of that. In the deep, your feet no longer touch the bottom. And that is where faith becomes real.

Just as I had to travel far offshore to even have the opportunity to catch something significant, God often leads us into places that feel beyond our control.

Not to overwhelm us. But to transform us.

To teach us how to depend on Him.
To learn how to float when we cannot stand.
To move with the current of His Spirit rather than resist it.

That day, I did not come home with a trophy fish. But I did come home with a revelation.

You cannot live a deep life with shallow faith**.**

"I am tormented with an everlasting itch for things remote. I love to sail forbidden seas, and land on barbarous coasts."
— Herman Melville, Moby-Dick

I have never read *Moby-Dick* from cover to cover, nor have I sat through a full film adaptation. And yet, somehow, this story has followed me over the years. It has appeared in sermons, surfaced in leadership books, and been referenced in conversations about purpose and obsession. That is the mark of a true classic. It finds its way into your world even if you have never opened its pages.

There is a particular line from the book that has always stirred something in me: "I am tormented with an everlasting itch for things remote."

It feels like more than a line about the sea. It feels like a window into the human soul.

It is interesting how a story I have never fully explored has still managed to name something within me. The restless part. The part that refuses to be satisfied with the safety of the shore.

That line is where I want to pause. Because sometimes that is all we need in a season. Not the whole story, but a single sentence that exposes what has been quietly living inside us.

"I am tormented with an everlasting itch for things remote."

That is more than a sailor's longing to explore. It is the human spirit reaching for something beyond what is near and familiar.

We may not all chase whales across open oceans, but each of us carries an ache for something deeper. Something holier. Something less contained.

It is the desire for purpose that cannot be satisfied with shallow living. It is the quiet pull that wakes you in the middle of the night and reminds you that there is more.

The itch does not go away. And perhaps it is not meant to.

Wild faith does not only appear in moments of clarity or worship. It often pulls at us from the edges. From the distant, unfinished, and unknown spaces of our lives.

It is what draws us out of the boat.

It is what keeps us from settling.

It is what leads us into the deep.

So no, I have not read *Moby-Dick*. But in some ways, I have lived that line. Maybe you have too. And maybe that is the point.

Sometimes all it takes is a single sentence to call us beyond the horizon, into the wild unknown where God is already waiting.

Beyond the Horizon: The Call of the Wild Unknown

Wild faith does not stop at the shoreline. It calls you to places maps cannot chart and logic cannot comfort. It is not just about believing when things make sense. It is about walking, swimming, and surrendering when they do not.

The horizon has always represented the edge of what is known. For the ancient world, it marked the line between life and mystery, between safety and surrender. Sailors once feared they would fall off the edge of the earth if they dared to cross it. But for those willing to go, the horizon was not a boundary. It was a beginning.

And so it is with wild faith. There comes a moment when God invites you to move beyond the faith that has carried you this far. The prayers you have prayed. The paths you have walked. The ways you have known Him. It is not that those things were wrong. It is that they are no longer sufficient for where He is leading you.

The same shallow waters that once felt sacred can begin to feel stagnant. Your soul starts to crave more than survival.

It wants to swim. In Ezekiel's vision, the river flowing from the temple deepens step by step. First ankle deep. Then knee deep. Then waist deep. And finally, it becomes a river no one can cross, a place where the only option is to stop walking and begin swimming.

This is what it means to go into the deep. This is what wild faith invites. Full surrender.

No more feet on the bottom.

No more control over the current.

Only trust.

It is unsettling.

It is beautiful.

It is holy.

And it is where transformation happens. The wild unknown is not about recklessness. It is about release. It is about discovering that faith was never meant to be controlled, but lived. Fully. Freely. Reverently.

It is where your plans begin to loosen their grip and God's possibilities begin to unfold. It is where striving gives way to trust. Where you stop trying to hold everything together and begin to rest in the reality that you are already being held.

The world teaches you to build a life you can manage. Wild faith invites you to live a life that requires God. So consider the question honestly.

What is your horizon? What edge have you been unwilling to cross? What would it look like to take the step, to trust, to move beyond what feels secure? Because the deep is not empty. God is already there. Waiting.

As Deep Cries Out to Deep

There comes a moment when the soul begins to ache, not from pain, but from longing. A yearning that is difficult to explain, yet impossible to ignore. It is the stirring of the Spirit within you, calling out to the Spirit of God.

The psalmist gives voice to this longing:

"Deep calls to deep in the roar of your waterfalls; all your waves and breakers have swept over me."

(Psalm 42:7)

This is not surface-level faith. This is the cry of a soul that has tasted shallow water and found it insufficient. It is the response of a heart that can no longer be satisfied with routine.

There are seasons when what once stirred you begins to feel quiet. The songs that once moved you. The sermons that once inspired you. The rhythms that once sustained you. They no longer reach the same depth.

It is not because something is wrong. It is because something deeper is calling. Safe patterns can begin to feel restrictive. What once felt like structure can start to feel like confinement. And in that tension, God begins to whisper: There is more.

"Deep calls to deep" is an invitation into communion that moves beyond understanding. It is an invitation to encounter God not only in clarity, but also in mystery. Not only in answered prayers, but also in silence. Not only on the mountaintop, but in the places you once believed were too dark or distant to be reached.

It is in the deep that you begin to discover who God truly is.

And who you are in Him. In the deep, titles lose their meaning. Comfort has no place to stand. Pretense falls away, and what remains is real.

Your hunger. Your questions. Your surrender. And there, in that place, God does not always answer with explanations. He answers with Himself.

When your deep ache meets His deep presence, something sacred unfolds. It is not always dramatic or overwhelming. Sometimes it is quiet. Steady. Certain.

A knowing that settles beneath the noise. You are not alone. He is enough. Even here, you are held. So let the deep within you cry out. Let your thirst be expressed. Let your soul lean, long, and listen.

Because the God of the deep is not intimidated by your questions, your doubts, or your desire. These are not obstacles to Him. They are often the very places where He meets you most personally. He is not confined to the heights. He meets you in the depths.

The North Atlantic Current

In the natural world, one of the most powerful forces shaping life across continents is the North Atlantic Current. It is not loud, and it is rarely seen, yet it is essential. Flowing from the Gulf of Mexico and curving across the Atlantic toward Europe, this deep ocean current carries warm water thousands of miles. It regulates climate, sustains ecosystems, and makes life possible in regions that would otherwise freeze.

It does all of this beneath the surface. Steadily. Faithfully. Unseen.

You cannot observe it unless you are intentionally looking for it. You may not feel it immediately. Yet it is always there, moving, guiding, sustaining.

In many ways, the North Atlantic Current reflects how God moves through time and space. Just as the current travels across oceans, unseen yet transformative, God **is at work** through history, guiding His purposes, warming cold seasons, and directing the flow of our lives, even when we **cannot perceive** it. Unlike us, God **is not confined** by time. We live moment by moment, carried along by the present. But God stands beyond it. He is not subject to time. He created it.

Isaiah 46:10 declares, "I make known the end from the beginning, from ancient times, what is still to come."

He sees the full expanse of your life, from your first breath to your final moment. If we could see with His perspective, doubt would lose its power. Just as the warmth carried by the Atlantic current eventually transforms distant shores, the work of God in your life today may not fully reveal itself until tomorrow, or even in eternity. Yet nothing is wasted.

Not a single wave.
Not a single delay.
Not a single prayer whispered through tears.

He is the God of the deep. The God of hidden currents that carry us forward even when we feel ***still****.*

When life feels slow or silent, remember the North Atlantic. Something is always moving beneath the surface. God is never inactive. He is never forgetful. He is never late.

And just as that current carries life across oceans, so the Spirit of God carries you through every season, across every storm, into places He has already seen.

As we have journeyed through the deep waters of trust, time, and unseen movement, one truth rises clearly above the waves.

God is always moving, even when you are waiting. The deeper you walk with Him, the more you begin to realize that this is not a single moment of surrender. It is a lifelong pursuit.

Deep faith does not only anchor you. It awakens you. It sharpens your awareness. It tunes your spirit to the quiet rhythm of God's activity beneath the surface of everyday life. And if you begin to listen closely, you will notice it.

The whisper. The nudge. The invitation. Now is the moment.

In the next chapter, we will explore what it means to live **attentive** and awake. To recognize God's invitations in real time. To walk with spiritual urgency. To say yes not only in profound moments, but in ordinary ones. Because wild faith is not only about going deep.It is about staying ready.

Coaching Reflection

You were created for more than the shallow end. Wild faith is not content to remain near the shore, where control feels comfortable and the bottom is always visible. Deep faith trusts God enough to move beyond sight, beyond certainty, and beyond what seems logically secure.

But going deeper requires surrender. It means releasing control and trusting the One who sees the full ocean, not just your present current. You may not understand the timing or the direction of the tide, but you can trust the One who governs both.

So pause and consider:

- Am I still trying to stand where God is inviting me to swim?
- Have I mistaken comfort for calling?
- What fear or resistance is keeping me from moving into deeper waters of wild faith?

Remember this truth:

The deeper you go, the more you rely not on your own strength, but on His presence.

Coaching Insight

The Big Truth

Deep faith is not about intensity. It is about trust. Going deeper with God does not mean doing more or striving harder. It means surrendering control and learning to rely on His presence when certainty fades. The deep is not dangerous when God is the One who invites you there. It is where faith matures, identity settles, and intimacy grows.

The Mirror Question

Where are you still trying to keep your feet on the bottom when God is inviting you to swim? What part of your faith feels shallow, not because it is wrong, but because you have outgrown it?

The Thirty First Footstep

Name one area of your life where you are clinging to visibility, certainty, or control. Identify one small act of trust that moves you deeper rather than safer. This is not a dramatic leap. It is a willing release. Deep faith begins when you stop standing and allow yourself to be carried.

The Inner Work

Moving into the deep often awakens fear, grief, and resistance. You may miss the familiarity of routines that once sustained you. You may feel exposed without clear footing. These reactions are not signs that you are failing. They are signs that you are transitioning. The deep strips away performance and invites presence. God is not asking you to prove your faith. He is inviting you to trust Him beyond what you can manage or measure. When control loosens, dependence grows. When dependence grows, intimacy follows.

Reflection Prompt

What emotions surface when you imagine releasing control and trusting God without knowing the outcome? Where do you sense a quiet longing for more depth, even if you cannot yet name what that looks like?

Prayer of Alignment

God, I confess that I often prefer shallow waters where I feel safe and capable. Teach me to trust You in the deep. Help me release the need to see the bottom and rest in Your presence instead. When fear rises, steady me. When control tempts me, remind me that You are already holding me. I choose surrender over certainty and trust over comfort. Lead me deeper, one faithful step at a time. Amen.

Chapter 9: On Mission Every Day

Living Wild Beyond Sunday
Your Red Pill Moment

"You take the red pill, you stay in Wonderland, and I show you how deep the rabbit hole goes."

— Morpheus, The Matrix

There is a moment in *The Matrix* that changed cinema and, for many people, changed the way they saw their own lives. It is the moment when Morpheus offers Neo a choice. The blue pill represents comfort, routine, and forgetfulness. The red pill offers a wild and uncertain journey into truth, risk, and transformation.

Morpheus was not simply inviting Neo to see reality. He was inviting him into purpose. I still remember sitting in a dark movie theater watching *The Matrix* for the first time. I did not fully understand everything I was seeing, but I felt something shift inside me. It was more than action. More than special effects. There was a weight to it, a tension that stayed with me long after the credits rolled.

I walked out unsettled. Awake in a way I could not yet explain. The idea that there might be more happening beneath the surface of everyday life stirred something deep within me. The thought that a person could wake up, see reality for what it truly is, and never go back left me both fascinated and uneasy. I did not yet have language for it, but I felt the pull of a question that would follow me for years:

What if there is more?

And what if, once you see it, you are responsible to respond?

"Unfortunately, no one can be told what the Matrix is. You must see it for yourself."

Morpheus, *The Matrix*

In many ways, wild faith works the same way. It is not something you can merely explain, memorize, or confine to Sundays. It must be lived. It must be stepped into. Every morning, God extends an invitation:

Will you keep living safe and predictable? Or will you step into a reality where every moment is charged with meaning, possibility, and mission?

Living on mission every day is our red pill moment. It means waking up to a world that is far bigger than paychecks, chores, and the status quo. It means becoming aware of the spiritual battles unfolding around us, the opportunities to serve, the invitation to love boldly, and the adventure God has woven into even the most ordinary hours.

It means refusing to hit snooze on your calling. In *The Matrix*, Neo could not unsee what was real. Once his eyes were opened, he had to respond. In Christ, once we begin to see who God is and what He is doing all around us, passive faith is no longer enough.

Wild faith pulls us into the story of God. It invites us to partner with Him at work, at home, in our neighborhoods, and in the hidden spaces of everyday life.

So what does that look like in practice?

- You begin to realize that every conversation could become a Kingdom moment.
- Your everyday work becomes an act of worship and witness.
- Interruptions begin to look like divine appointments.
- You live awake to the needs, wounds, and hopes around you, ready to respond in faith.

When you choose wild faith, you choose to see and to serve. To risk and to love. To bring light into places you never expected. That is what it means to live on mission every day.

Wild faith comes alive not only in what we pray, but in how we live, day after day. Faith that remains in our thoughts, journals, or intentions never changes the world. But when we begin to live as though God is telling the truth, the adventure truly begins.

Living Awake to Mission

To live on mission is to live awake. It is more than participating in a short term trip or volunteering at a church event, though those things matter. Living on mission means aligning your life with a greater purpose that extends beyond comfort, productivity, or even success. You begin to see your time, your gifts, and your everyday rhythms through the lens of eternity.

You are no longer waiting for a pulpit or a platform. You realize your life is the platform. When you live on mission, your home becomes a sanctuary. Your table becomes a place of fellowship. Your job becomes a field where the Kingdom can break through.

You are not simply going to work, raising children, or running errands. You are representing Christ in every space you enter, whether you are aware of it or not.

Living on mission requires awareness. It is not about doing more. It is about doing what you are already doing with intention and purpose. When you are living on mission, something begins to shift.

You see people differently.

- That difficult coworker becomes a soul worth loving.

- That stranger at the coffee shop becomes someone God is already pursuing.
- You approach tasks with intention.

Even the smallest actions, writing an email, folding laundry, leading a meeting, become opportunities to reflect the character of God.

- You stay spiritually attentive.
- You begin to listen for the Holy Spirit throughout your day.
- You notice gentle nudges.
- You pause before speaking.
- You pray in moments that do not require closing your eyes.

You take ownership.

You stop outsourcing your spiritual life to a Sunday service or waiting for someone else to disciple you.

You recognize that you carry the fire, and it is your responsibility to keep it burning. The mission field is not a location.

It is a posture.

It is showing up with open hands and asking, "Lord, what do You want to do through me here?"

You do not need to be known to be effective. You do not need to be loud to be powerful.

You need to be available.

Some of the most significant movements of God begin quietly, with someone saying yes.

Yes to the nudge to reach out.

Yes to the whisper to stop and pray.

Yes to walking across the room.

Yes to planting seeds that may never be seen.

Living on mission is not about arrival.

It is about attention.

It is about noticing.

Noticing the pain in someone's eyes.

Noticing the fear in their voice.

Noticing the opportunity hidden inside what looks like an interruption.

It is about remembering.

Remembering that you are an ambassador of a Kingdom.

A carrier of the Spirit.

A reflection of Jesus in every place you go.

You may never travel across the world.

But you can bring the culture of heaven into your home.

You may never stand on a stage.

But you can lead your family with vision, patience, and love.

You may not feel courageous.

But every time you choose obedience over avoidance, you are living on mission.

Awake and Available: Living Your Yes

Here is the truth: you do not drift into living on mission.

You decide into it.

It is easy to become numb to the divine. The daily grind, the weight of responsibility, and the distractions of comfort can slowly lull even the most passionate heart to sleep. But wild faith wakes you up. It lifts your eyes. It reminds you that you were never created merely to exist.

You were created to impact.

You do not have to wait until you feel ready. In fact, living on mission rarely begins when you feel equipped. It begins when you say yes, even when your voice shakes.

When you begin to live with a yes in your spirit, everything starts to change.

Interruptions become invitations.

Detours become divine.

Errands become encounters.

Slowly, the sacred begins to spill into the ordinary.

That moment in traffic becomes a time of intercession.

That casual conversation at work becomes a place of empathy.

That neighborhood walk becomes a prayer walk.

That moment of weakness becomes a testimony of strength.

Living on mission is not about having a title or a microphone.

It is about being awake and available.

It is about seeing what others miss and moving when others hesitate.

You become a yes on two legs.

A walking, breathing answer to the brokenness around you.

Not perfect.

Not impressive.

Just willing.

And willing is enough.

Living your yes does not mean saying yes to everything.

It means saying yes to the right things.

It is a posture of availability, a way of living that tells God, "Whatever You are doing today, I want to be part of it."

This kind of yes is rarely loud or dramatic. More often, it is hidden in the margins of ordinary life.

It looks like making the phone call when you would rather scroll.

It looks like lingering in a conversation when you are already running late.

It looks like opening your door when you are tired.

It looks like offering encouragement when your own heart feels heavy. Yes does not wait for perfect conditions. It moves in obedience even when the path is unclear.

***To live your yes is to live both** anchored and surrendered.*

Anchored in the truth of God, because wild faith must be rooted somewhere deep.

Surrendered to the pace of God, because His timing often interrupts our own.

And if we are honest, your yes will cost you something.

But what it gives in return is far greater.

Clarity.

Joy.

Purpose.

And the deep thrill of walking in step with the Spirit of God.

Your yes will reshape how you pray.

It will open space in your calendar for people.

It will stretch your compassion.

It will get under your skin in the best possible way and awaken parts of you that fear once tried to bury.

Living your yes is not about becoming extra spiritual.

It is about becoming more surrendered.

And that yes compounds over time.

A life of bold faith is not built in one dramatic moment. It is built brick by brick, moment by moment, yes by yes.

Some days your yes will feel courageous.

Other days it will feel costly.

But every yes, when offered in faith, becomes sacred.

No More Negotiating

There comes a moment, whether quiet or thunderous, when you realize you have spent too much of your life in conversation with fear.

You have sat at the table with doubt.

You have offered compromise to anxiety.

You have waited for insecurity to approve your next step.

You may have called it wisdom.

Caution.

Even spiritual discernment.

But the truth is, you have been negotiating with something that was never meant to have a voice in your destiny.

Fear does not negotiate.

It delays.

It distracts.

It keeps you circling decisions without ever stepping fully into them.

At first, it can feel responsible. You tell yourself you are being thoughtful. That you are praying more. That you are waiting on God.

But often, you are not waiting on God.

You are waiting for fear to become quiet.

And it never does.

In fact, fear often grows loudest right before you are about to step into something God has ordained.

It disguises itself as maturity.

But in reality, it is captivity.

There comes a time when faith must draw a line in the sand.

Enough rehearsing the what ifs.

Enough doubting what God has already confirmed.

Enough bowing to hesitation while heaven is saying, Go.

Wild faith does not wait for fear to leave the room.

It moves forward in spite of it.

Not with arrogance.

But with a trembling, resolute yes.

That is the turning point.

The moment you say:

I am done waiting for the absence of fear.

I am choosing to move with the presence of God.

That is when everything begins to change.

You stop overanalyzing.

You stop asking for twelve more confirmations.

You stop asking fear for permission to live boldly.

And instead, you remember.

You remember the last time God showed up.

The last time He made a way.

The last time obedience, not comfort, led to breakthrough.

You stop crowdsourcing your calling.

You stop negotiating with your limitations.

You stop demanding clarity before commitment.

Because clarity often comes after obedience, not before it.

No more negotiating with the fear of not being enough.

God never asked you to be enough.

He asked you to be available.

No more negotiating with the need to control outcomes.

Obedience is not rooted in guarantees.

It is rooted in trust.

No more negotiating with what other people might think.

If Moses had waited for consensus, Israel would still be in chains.

When you stop negotiating with fear, something breaks open inside of you.

You breathe deeper.

You stand taller.

You stop tiptoeing around your purpose.

You stop deferring your calling to a future season that never arrives.

And you begin to walk with a wild, holy confidence.

Not confidence in yourself. Confidence in the One who called you.

Because what fear has been trying to protect you from was never worth the price of disobedience.

You do not need another fleece.

You need to decide.

You do not need to feel brave.

You need to be willing.

You do not need to solve everything.

You need to say yes.

No more explaining.

No more stalling.

No more bowing to invisible barriers.

No more negotiating with fear.

Just raw.

Real.

Wild obedience.

Step out and trust that God will meet you in the going.

"If you hear a voice within you say, 'you cannot paint,' then by all means paint, and that voice will be silenced."
— Vincent Van Gogh

Carrying the Presence: A Life Lived as a Sanctuary

To carry the presence of God is to move through life as a living sanctuary.

It is a soul made aware.

A life spiritually attuned.

A heart held open to the Divine in the middle of ordinary moments.

This kind of life is not reserved for pulpits, prayer rooms, or Sunday mornings.

It happens in checkout lines and on morning commutes.

At kitchen sinks and in hospital waiting rooms.

In classrooms, break rooms, parking lots, and quiet corners of everyday life.

You carry Him not because of your perfection, but because of your consecration.

As 2 Corinthians 4:7 reminds us, "We have this treasure in jars of clay, to show that the surpassing power belongs to God and not to us."

You have said yes.

You have made room.

You have allowed your life to become more than a schedule.

It has become a vessel.

The Spirit no longer dwells in temples made by human hands.

He dwells in surrendered people.

Acts 17:24–25 reminds us, "The God who made the world and everything in it… does not live in temples built by human hands. And

He is not served by human hands, as if He needed anything. Rather, He Himself gives everyone life and breath and everything else."

The more you acknowledge His nearness, the more aware you become of His movement.

A whispered prayer before a conversation.

A pause before a reaction.

A quiet prompting to speak.

A gentle restraint to remain silent.

All of these moments become sacred when you realize He is with you in them.

Your awareness becomes an altar.

Your obedience becomes an offering.

To carry His presence means learning to guard the flame He has lit within you.

Paul told Timothy in 2 Timothy 1:6, "Fan into flame the gift of God, which is in you."

That means protecting your peace.

Turning down the noise of the world.

Making space to hear the still, small voice of God again.

It means paying attention, not only to your own inner life, but also to what God may be doing in the atmosphere around you.

When you carry His presence, interruptions begin to look different.

Interruptions become invitations.

Strangers become divine appointments.

Silence becomes a form of worship.

And perhaps most importantly, carrying His presence is less about striving and more about staying.

Staying close.

Staying available.

Staying rooted in love.

Jesus said in John 15:4, "Abide in Me, and I in you. As the branch cannot bear fruit of itself unless it abides in the vine, neither can you unless you abide in Me."

To abide in Him is to carry Him.

And when you begin to live this way, everything becomes holy ground.

Not because of where you are.

But because of who is in you.

The sacred does not wait for Sunday.

It appears whenever a willing heart walks into the room and brings heaven with it.

"You cannot live a fearless life until you've given up on a safe one"
— Erwin Raphael McManus

Eyes Wide Open to the Sacred

This is the essence of carrying the presence of God.

To truly live with spiritual awareness, with your eyes wide open, you must be willing to enter spaces others avoid. You must release safe religion, predictable comfort, and invisible living. You must be willing to carry light into darkness, not because you are fearless, but because God is with you.

We do not carry His presence only when we feel strong.

We do not carry Him only when we feel worthy.

We carry Him because we said yes.

We carry Him into boardrooms and break rooms. Into dinner tables and detention centers. Into classrooms and quiet hospital rooms.

And when we do, we begin to walk through life with our eyes wide open to the sacred moments hidden inside ordinary days.

The more aware you become of His nearness, the more you begin to notice what others often miss.

The quiet ache in a coworker's voice.

The subtle prompting to pray for someone passing by.

The courage to speak peace when tension fills the room.

You begin to move differently.

You become a holy disruption to fear.

The presence of God is not reserved for Sunday services or mountaintop moments.

It is in you.

With you.

Working through you.

Right now.

You do not need to strive to bring Him in.

You need only to become aware.

And say yes.

The Mission Is Now

You do not have to wait for a pulpit, a platform, or the perfect opportunity to begin living on mission.

If Christ is in you, then every moment already carries the potential for holiness.

Every hallway can become a place of encounter.

Every ordinary task can become a sacred act.

The true adventure of wild faith is not found only in the epic leaps.

It is found in the daily steps.

It is found in choosing presence over distraction.

Purpose over passivity.

Trust over fear.

To live on mission every day is to live fully awake.

It is to recognize that the Kingdom of God is not only coming.

It is already here.

Jesus said, "The kingdom of God is within you" (Luke 17:21).

That means we are not simply waiting for revival.

We are meant to carry it.

The red pill has already been offered.

The invitation has already been extended.

You have already tasted what it means to come alive in Christ.

Now live it.

Not someday.

Not when you feel more qualified.

Not when it becomes easier.

Not when it feels safer.

Now.

Because the world is not waiting for more polished Christians.

It is aching for people marked by wild, surrendered faith.

People who walk what they believe.

People who shine in dark places.

People who carry the presence and fire of God into spaces only they can reach.

This is your moment. This is your mission.

Prayer

Father, awaken me to Your nearness.

Teach me to walk with my eyes wide open, aware of Your Spirit, attentive to Your whisper, and willing to carry Your presence wherever I go.

Let my life become a light in dark places, not by my own strength, but by Your power at work within me.

Use my words, my choices, my interruptions, and my ordinary moments for Your glory. Help me live awake, available, and unafraid.

Amen.

Declaration

Today, I say yes.

I carry the presence of God.

I am not invisible.

I am not passive.

I am not afraid.

I walk with purpose.

I speak with love.

I live aware of the sacred in every step.

Where I go, the Kingdom goes.

Because Christ lives in me.

"Not by might nor by power, but by My Spirit," says the Lord of Hosts.
— Zechariah 4:6

Coaching Insight

The Big Truth

Living on mission is not about doing more for God. It is about living aware of God.

Wild faith awakens you to the reality that your everyday life is already sacred ground. You are not waiting to be sent. You have already been placed.

Mission does not begin when conditions are ideal. It begins when awareness replaces autopilot and obedience replaces hesitation.

The Mirror Question

Where have you been compartmentalizing your faith instead of carrying it into everyday moments?

What part of your daily life have you quietly labeled as ordinary that God may be calling sacred?

The Thirty First Footstep

Choose one ordinary rhythm of your life where you tend to move on autopilot, such as work conversations, errands, family routines, or digital habits.

Enter that space with intention. Pray before you step into it. Ask God to help you remain awake and available rather than rushed or distracted.

Mission grows when awareness becomes practice.

The Inner Work

Living on mission often surfaces fear of visibility, fear of interruption, and fear of inadequacy.

You may feel pressure to perform or to say the right thing.

These fears often reveal an underlying belief that mission depends on your strength rather than God's presence.

You are not called to be impressive. You are called to be present.

God works through willingness more than confidence. When you stop negotiating with fear and begin responding to God's nearness, your life becomes a quiet testimony of faithfulness.

Reflection Prompt

What changes when you begin to see your daily life as a place where God is already at work?

Where do you notice resistance to staying spiritually awake in ordinary moments?

Prayer of Alignment

God, awaken me to Your nearness in the ordinary.

Teach me to recognize the holy moments woven into everyday life. I release the need to feel qualified or fearless. I choose availability over comfort and obedience over delay.

Help me carry Your presence with humility, courage, and love wherever I go. Let my yes become an offering that brings Your Kingdom near.

Amen

Chapter 10: Passing the Torch

How to Ignite Faith in the Next Generation

"The legacy you leave is the life you live."
— *Like Arrows (2018)*

Faith That Was Never Meant to Stop With Us

Up to this point, we have seen how wild faith awakens us, how it calls us to risk, and how it refines us through fire. We have walked through moments where obedience cost something real and where trusting God required us to release control.

But wild faith was never meant to end with personal breakthrough or private devotion.

Faith that truly lives always looks beyond itself.

It looks for hands to pass into.

Hearts to ignite.

Lives to shape beyond its original spark.

Legacy is not built in one defining moment.

It is formed through daily surrender.

It is shaped by how we pray when no one is watching.

How we respond when life becomes messy.

How we remain faithful when outcomes stay hidden.

You do not have to be perfect to pass on faith.

You only have to be willing to keep the flame burning.

The question is not whether you are leaving a legacy.

The question is what kind of legacy you are leaving.

Wild Faith That Shaped a Nation

Wild faith has never been confined to personal spirituality.

It has always shaped movements, cultures, and nations.

American history is filled with ordinary people who believed obedience to God mattered more than comfort.

The Pilgrims crossed the Atlantic not because the journey was safe, but because worship without compromise was worth the risk. They faced storms, sickness, hunger, and devastating loss. Many did not survive the first winter.

Yet those who remained still gathered to pray and give thanks, believing that faithfulness mattered even when survival felt uncertain.

In the generations that followed, revival after revival swept across the colonies.

The First Great Awakening stirred hearts through the preaching of men like Jonathan Edwards and George Whitefield. Fields and meetinghouses filled with people hungry for God.

These gatherings did more than transform churches.

They shaped conscience. Conviction. Courage.

And they helped form the spiritual atmosphere of a growing nation.

Wild faith also became a force for justice.

Harriet Tubman trusted God not only for her own freedom, but for the freedom of others. She returned again and again into danger because obedience outweighed fear.

Frederick Douglass spoke truth at great personal cost, convinced that God's justice demanded action.

Later, during the Civil Rights Movement, Dr. Martin Luther King Jr. carried a faith rooted in Scripture, sacrifice, and holy conviction. He trusted that love could outlast hatred and that obedience could bend history.

Faith does not remain theoretical for long. When it is alive, it moves.

A Hunger That Refused to Stay Quiet

As I reflect on these moments in our nation's story, I recognize a familiar heartbeat.

Long before I understood it, I was standing in the current of something older and deeper.

The prayers whispered in small Oklahoma sanctuaries were echoes of a hunger carried across generations.

The people who came before us were not trying to start movements or build institutions.

They were responding to a longing they could not silence.

They wanted more than polished religion.

They wanted the presence of God.

They believed obedience mattered more than comfort.

Surrender mattered more than control.

They gathered in homes.

They prayed without agendas.

They waited without timelines.

And in those quiet moments of humility and hunger, faith was stripped of performance and reduced to dependence.

That hunger eventually found a place. And it found a name.

The Azusa Street Revival

At the dawn of the twentieth century, in a modest home on Bonnie Brae Street in Los Angeles, the fire that had been carried quietly through prayer burst into open flame.

The house was small.

The rooms were crowded.

The people were ordinary.

They came not for recognition, but for God.

Night after night, they gathered to pray, fast, and wait. There was no program to manage and no desire to control the outcome.

The only agenda was surrender.

William J. Seymour led these gatherings with deep humility. Often, he would pray quietly with his head buried in a wooden crate, convinced that if anything lasting was going to happen, God Himself would have to be the One to do it. And He did.

On April 9, 1906, the presence of God fell in a way that could not be contained.

People were filled with the Holy Spirit.

Worship erupted without prompting.

Repentance flowed freely.

Lives were marked forever.

What had once been whispered in prayer suddenly became visible.

The crowds grew.

Skeptics came. And many left transformed.

When the porch of the Bonnie Brae home collapsed under the weight of those gathering, the meetings moved to an abandoned building on Azusa Street.

There were no polished pulpits.

No rehearsed music.

No carefully controlled hierarchy.

Men and women, young and old, Black, white, and brown worshiped side by side in a unity that challenged the social boundaries of the time.

Some mocked what they could not understand.

Newspapers ridiculed the meetings.

Critics dismissed the movement.

But the fire did not fade.

It spread.

The Fire That Kept Moving

What ignited on Azusa Street did not remain confined to one building, one city, or one generation.

The fire spread because people carried it. Men and women who encountered the Holy Spirit returned home changed. They did not return with a polished script or a strategic blueprint.

They returned with conviction. Prayer meetings began to form in storefronts and living rooms across Chicago, New York, and the American South. In the Appalachian Mountains, small holiness gatherings erupted with renewed hunger. Across the Midwest, farmers and factory workers gathered after long days of labor to pray with the expectancy that God was still near and still moving.

What unified these movements was not structure.

It was surrender.

People were not chasing a name or building a platform.

They were responding to what they had encountered.

And the fire did not stop at the borders of the United States.

The ripple continued across the world.

Missionaries carried the flame to Europe, Latin America, Africa, and Asia. In Scandinavia, prayer movements emphasized repentance and Spirit-led living. In India, Pentecostal fellowships emerged among the poor and marginalized, marked by healing, prayer, and deep dependence on God. In Korea, early revival movements centered around all-night prayer and fasting, helping shape one of the most vibrant Christian movements in the world.

None of these expressions looked exactly the same. But they carried the same spiritual DNA.

Hunger.

Obedience.

Expectation.

Later movements followed the same pattern.

The Jesus People Movement of the 1960s and 1970s saw young people, disillusioned with religion but desperate for meaning, encounter God in homes, on beaches, and in small gatherings. Worship was raw. Testimony was personal. Scripture came alive. Many churches, missions organizations, and worship movements today still trace their roots back to that season of renewal.

Other revivals followed.

In Brownsville.

In Toronto.

And in countless lesser-known places that may never appear in history books. People gathered not to recreate Azusa, but to seek God with the same posture.

Some of those movements lasted for years.

Others faded quietly.

But all of them left a mark.

They formed people.

They deepened prayer lives.

They reignited hunger.

They sent believers back into the world with greater courage and deeper faith.

God rarely repeats the same expression.

But He always honors the same posture.

When people humble themselves, hunger for His presence, and choose obedience over comfort, movement follows. The legacy of Azusa Street is not trapped in history books or denominational timelines.

It lives wherever people seek God without conditions and carry the fire forward without needing recognition. Wild faith has always moved this way.

Quietly at first.

Then courageously.

Then irresistibly.

And every generation is given the same invitation:

Will you receive the fire only for yourself?

Or will you carry it forward so someone else can find their way to the flame?

A Faith Handed to Our Family

This is the faith I grew up around.

It was not polished.

It was not performed for show.

It was lived.

I watched it take shape in prayer circles that felt ordinary at the time and in quiet acts of obedience that never made headlines. It showed up in small sanctuaries filled with sincerity.

Around family tables where prayers were simple, but real. In whispered moments with God when no one else was listening.

Long before I had language for it, that wild faith was already shaping me. It was carried faithfully by people who believed God was still moving and still worth trusting.

They passed it on without fully realizing how deeply it would take root. Now I find myself standing in that same current, holding the same flame. And the question is no longer distant. It is personal.

What will I do with what has been entrusted to me?

How will I carry it forward?

How will I live in a way that keeps the fire burning for those watching now and for those still to come?

Our Wild Faith Journey

My wife and I have walked a road that has not always made sense on paper. It has been shaped by calling and cost.

By moments when obedience felt unmistakably clear and other moments when it felt painfully quiet.

Campus ministry and group homes.

Church planting and closed doors.

Seasons where fruit seemed to appear overnight and seasons where it felt like nothing was happening at all.

We have known deep joy and real heartbreak. We have celebrated life and mourned loss.

We have carried hope with open hands and learned what it means to surrender plans we once believed were from God.

There were times when we wondered whether we had heard Him clearly.

Times when faith felt strong.

Times when it felt thin.

And over time, we learned something important.

Wild faith does not protect you from disappointment.

It meets you there.

It does not promise ease.

It does not promise clarity.

It promises presence.

God has been with us in laughter and in grief, in certainty and in confusion.

And looking back now, I can see how every step was shaping us. Not only as leaders or ministers. But as parents.

The atmosphere our children are growing up in has been formed less by the faith we talked about and more by the faith we lived in front of them.

Legacy is not something you build later when life finally slows down.

It is something you are already living right now.

In how you pray.

In how you respond.

In how you stay faithful when answers take longer than expected.

Igniting Faith in the Next Generation

Wild faith multiplies when it is shared honestly, not perfectly.

Children learn how to pray by watching how we pray when we do not have the answers. They learn courage by watching us obey when it costs us something.

They learn trust by seeing us return to God again and again, even after disappointment, even after loss.

Sometimes passing the torch looks like telling our stories. Not the polished versions. The real ones.

Sometimes it looks like inviting others into prayer before we feel confident.

Sometimes it looks like allowing people to witness our faith while it is still being formed, before the ending is clear.

Your yes to God is never just for you.

It is for the people watching how you live it. It is for the children learning what faith looks like by how you respond when life does not go as planned.

It is for the next generation who will decide whether faith is worth trusting based on what they see in you.

The fire you carry was never meant to be hidden or protected behind perfection.

It was meant to be handed forward.

Even with trembling hands.

And now, the torch is in your hands.

Coaching Insight

The Big Truth

Legacy is not something you leave behind when your life is finished. It is something you are forming every day by how you live your faith in front of others.

Wild faith was never meant to be stored, protected, or admired from a distance. It was meant to be carried, embodied, and handed forward.

The next generation will not inherit your beliefs as much as they will absorb your posture.

They are learning what faith looks like by watching how you pray, how you repent, how you endure, and how you return to God when life does not go as planned.

You do not pass on faith by being impressive. You pass it on by being faithful.

The Mirror Question

Where is your faith being lived privately but not modeled publicly?

What moments in your everyday life are quietly shaping the spiritual imagination of those watching you?

If someone followed your example rather than your advice, what kind of faith would they learn?

The Thirty First Footstep

Identify one relationship where your faith is already being observed by someone younger or less experienced than you.

This may be a child, a family member, a student, or someone you influence without even realizing it.

Ask yourself:

What am I showing them about faith through the way I live? Then choose one simple way to make your faith more visible this week.

It may be inviting them into prayer, sharing a story of God's faithfulness, or allowing them to witness your trust in a difficult moment.

Legacy is formed in lived moments, not just spoken lessons.

The Inner Work

Passing the torch often surfaces fear.

Fear of failing.

Fear of being exposed.

Fear of not having enough faith to give away.

These fears reveal a misunderstanding of how legacy is formed.

You are not responsible for producing faith in the next generation.

You are responsible for carrying it honestly.

God does not ask you to hand off perfection.

He asks you to hand off presence.

When you stop trying to appear spiritually complete and start living faithfully incomplete, you create space for others to believe that God can meet them too.

Legacy is formed when faith is practiced in real time, not when it is performed in hindsight.

Reflection Prompt

What memories of faith shaped you before you ever understood theology or doctrine?

Where are you tempted to hide your faith rather than model it honestly?

What would it look like to trust God with how your faith story continues beyond you?

Prayer of Alignment

God, thank You for the faith that was handed to me before I even knew how to name it.

Thank You for the prayers, obedience, and courage of those who carried the fire long before I held it.

I release the pressure to be perfect and receive the responsibility to be faithful.

Help me live a faith worth passing on. Teach me to carry the flame with humility, honesty, and courage.

May those who come after me encounter You not only through my words, but through my life.

Amen.

Chapter 11:
The Wildest of Faith

Living Wild Faith with Eternity in Mind

"For the Christian, death is not the end of life but the gateway to eternity."

— Billy Graham

There is a kind of faith that does more than move mountains.

It reaches into eternity. It is the kind of faith that refuses to settle for what is merely seen and instead clings to what has been promised.

This is the wildest kind of faith. The faith that believes not only for healing, provision, or breakthrough in this life, but also for resurrection, for heaven, and for the unshakable hope of glory.

In a world that constantly screams **now**, wild faith dares to live for **forever**.

It is the kind of faith Abraham carried when he looked for a city whose builder and maker was God.

The kind of faith that sings in suffering. That stores treasure in heaven. That quietly declares, *This world is not my home.*

This kind of faith does not deny pain. It does not ignore loss. It does not pretend suffering is small.

It simply refuses to believe that death, disappointment, or delay get the final word. Eternal faith sees farther.

It anchors the soul when the temporary begins to shake. It steadies the heart when earthly things feel uncertain. It reminds us that what God has promised extends far beyond what this life can hold.

In this chapter, we will explore what it means to live with eyes fixed on eternity and why some of the wildest acts of faith are not always loud or visible, but quiet, steady, and enduring.

Sometimes the most radical faith is simply this: To keep believing that the best is still to come.

Eternity Talks Over Ice Cream

Not long ago, I was driving with my middle daughter on what had become one of our sweet little traditions, an ice cream run to our favorite local dairy store.

The sun was dipping low, casting golden streaks across the horizon, and the windows were rolled down, letting in the warm Oklahoma breeze. We had our usual orders, her Chocolate Chip Cookie Dough shake and my Peanut Butter Cup shake, and laughter flowed easily as we settled into the kind of simple joy that only ice cream and unhurried time together can bring.

But then, as often happens in those sacred in-between moments with your kids, the conversation turned deeper.

"Dad," she said softly, staring out the window, "do you ever think about heaven? Like… what happens when we die? Sometimes I get scared thinking about forever. It's just… so big. So scary."

I glanced over at her, her face lit by the fading light and the flicker of innocent fear, and I felt that familiar ache a father knows well.

The ache of wanting to make everything safe. The ache of wanting to say something that removes every fear.

But I also knew this was a holy moment.

This was not a question to brush aside with a cliché or rush past with easy reassurance.

So, with ice cream still in hand and my eyes still on the road, I turned my heart fully toward her.

"Yes," I told her, "I do think about it. Heaven and eternity are big. Bigger than our minds can fully understand. But here's what gives me peace. It's not the idea of forever that comforts me. It's Who I'll be with forever."

Her eyes met mine, and I kept going.

"When Jesus said, 'I go to prepare a place for you,' He meant it. And when we believe in Him, eternity is not something we have to fear. It's a promise we can look forward to. I don't know all the details, but I trust the One who does."

She didn't say much right away.

She just nodded slowly,

And somehow, that was enough.

A small seed of peace had been planted.

That conversation with my daughter stayed with me long after the ice cream was gone.

Not because I had all the answers, but because it reminded me how deeply even young hearts wrestle with eternal questions.

And maybe that is part of the mystery of wild faith.

It does not eliminate every question.

It anchors us when the answers are still beyond us.

Jesus said in Matthew 18:3, *"Truly I tell you, unless you change and become like little children, you will never enter the kingdom of heaven."*

For a long time, I assumed that meant innocence or simplicity.

And maybe, in part, it does.

But sitting in that truck, I realized something deeper.

Childlike faith is not the absence of hard questions.

It is the willingness to ask them and still choose to trust the Father anyway.

It is not pretending we are never afraid of eternity.

It is knowing who holds eternity and believing that He is good.

That is our role, especially as parents, leaders, and spiritual mentors.

Not to have airtight theological explanations for every mystery.

Not to offer foolproof timelines or polished certainty.

But to point people to the Person of Jesus.

To hold space for wonder and fear.

And then gently lead them back to the promise:

"Do not let your hearts be troubled…
In My Father's house are many rooms…
I go to prepare a place for you"

(John 14:1–3).

Wild faith does not only believe for miracles in the present. It also believes for the promise of forever. It says, "Even though I do not fully understand, I still trust You." It clings to the truth of 2 Corinthians 4:18:

"So we fix our eyes not on what is seen, but on what is unseen, since what is seen is temporary, but what is unseen is eternal."

That night in the truck, my daughter did not walk away with every anxiety erased. But she did walk away knowing she was not alone in her questions.

And more importantly, she walked away knowing that the One who made her had already written eternity on her heart.

This is the kind of legacy I want to leave. Not one built on flawless answers, but on courageous trust.

I want to raise my children to face eternity not with fear, but with wild, wide-eyed faith, knowing that our future is not a question mark.

It is a promise sealed by the One who conquered death.

Heaven on Our Mind

We were not made for this world alone.

Deep down, we all know it.

That restless ache. That longing for justice. That deep desire to see what is broken made whole.

It is the echo of eternity stirring in our bones. In a world that feels more unstable by the day, where headlines whisper threats of global conflict and prophetic signs seem to flash like warning lights, the question presses in with greater urgency:

Are we ready?

But being "rapture ready" is not about stockpiling fear or obsessing over dates.

It is not about escaping the world.

It is about living fully in this world while keeping our eyes fixed on the One who is coming back.

It is the steady confidence that no matter what shakes around us, we are anchored in the One who promised to return.

Jesus told us to **watch and pray** (Luke 21:36).

That is not a call to paranoia.

It is a call to purpose.

In days when earthquakes rumble, rumors of wars stir fear, and darkness seems to grow louder, those who have heaven on their minds do not shrink back. They rise up.

Paul wrote in Titus 2:13 that we are
"waiting for our blessed hope, the appearing of the glory of our great God and Savior, Jesus Christ."

That hope does not make us passive. It makes us urgent. It transforms how we live, how we love, and how we lead others.

Wild faith says:

"I may not know the day or the hour, but I know who is coming, and I want to be found faithful."

As nations shake and uncertainty grows, many are paralyzed by anxiety.

But the believer who has heaven on their mind lives differently.

They love deeper.
They speak truth with greater boldness.
They give more freely.
They disciple their children like eternity matters, because it does.

And not out of fear. Out of expectancy. Heaven is not just our destination. It is our orientation. We live today in light of forever.

We forgive like heaven is near.
We worship like the sky could split open.
We raise our children with eternity in mind.
We speak to people like souls matter, because they do.

Jesus is coming again. And when He does, the trumpet will sound, the sky will open, and everything we once thought was so important will suddenly fade in the brilliance of His return.

So let us live like it.

Let us be found with oil in our lamps (Matthew 25:1–13), hearts on fire, eyes lifted, and hands faithfully working the harvest. Being ready is not a posture of escape. It is a lifestyle of holy expectation.

Because the King is coming.

And we want to be ready, not only for ourselves, but for the generations behind us who are watching our faith and learning what hope looks like through how we live.

Living with heaven on our minds changes everything.

It realigns our priorities. It loosens our grip on temporary things. It tunes our hearts to the sound of eternity.

We begin to see the world not only for what it is, but for what it is becoming:

A new heaven and a new earth. A place where justice and joy will reign. A kingdom where Jesus Himself will be the light that never fades. But eternal hope is not only about preparing for what is ahead. It is also about how we endure the ache in the meantime. Because even with our eyes fixed on eternity, our hearts still break.

We still lose people we love. We still face diagnoses, funerals, and anniversaries that arrive too soon. And yet wild faith dares to believe that even in death, the story is not over.

This is where hope grows deepest. Not in the absence of sorrow, but in the presence of a Savior who has already gone before us through the veil.

The curtain was torn. The tomb was emptied. And the promise was made:

"Because I live, you also will live"

(John 14:19).

This is the hope we stand in now. So let us go there. Let us talk about what it means to grieve with hope. To face death not with denial, but with a faith so fierce it lights up the darkness.

To carry the torch of legacy forward while keeping our eyes fixed beyond the veil. Because wild faith does not merely survive the thought of eternity. It lives in light of it.

When Heaven Feels Closer

Sometimes heaven does not feel far away at all.

It brushes against us in moments of worship, in whispered prayers, and in the stories we tell of those we have loved and long to see again.

There are days when eternity feels as if it is just on the other side of the veil. And the veil feels paper-thin.

Earlier in this book, we paused to consider the image of the North Atlantic Current. I want to return to it here.

Not because it needs to be explained again, but because some metaphors deepen the longer you sit with them.

What once helped us understand movement can, over time, help us understand meaning.

Years ago, while completing required reading for one of my master's classes, I wrote an assessment paper that I recently stumbled across again. As I reread those old reflections, I was struck by something God revealed to me back then and has continued to clarify over time.

It felt like a Genesis moment. A glimpse into the mystery of how God exists both within time and beyond it.

God does not sit on His throne as a detached observer, watching history unfold from a distance like a spectator to a film.

He is not removed from our moments.

He steps in and out of what we call time. He uses our days, our senses, and even the smallest details of our lives to make Himself known and to prepare us for what is still ahead.

Picture the timeline of your life.

Birth. The long stretch of living. And then death.

Between those points are what I think of as sacred thresholds. Boundary moments that shape and define our story.

A wedding day.
The birth of a child.
The loss of someone we love.
A calling answered.
A door opened.
A door quietly closed.

Birth |-------------------|---------------------| Death

And this is where that familiar image returns.

Like the North Atlantic Current, God's movement is steady, powerful, and purposeful.

That current moves through the vast body of the ocean, shaping climates, carrying life, and sustaining ecosystems, all while remaining largely unseen.

It is not the whole ocean. But it influences everything it touches.

In much the same way, God is both within the current of time and beyond it. He holds the whole ocean in His hands. He sees the beginning and the end at once.

We, however, are carried along within the current, only able to see what is immediately in front of us. But God steps in and out at will.

He moves through our days, our prayers, our pain, and our progress with perfect timing. Psalm 139 reminds us that all our days were written in His book before one of them came to be.

God is not limited by time.

He authored it.

He meets us fully in the present while already holding our future.

That is sovereignty.

That is love.

That is why we can trust Him when storms rise and waves roar.

He is not surprised.
He is not scrambling.
He is not guessing.

He sees beyond what we can see. And through the Holy Spirit, He gives wisdom, strength, and peace as we are carried along the current.

Isaiah tells us that when we pass through the waters, He will be with us, and when we pass through the rivers, they will not sweep over us. His presence is not only ahead of us.

It is with us now.

In every transition.
In every threshold.
In every crossing.

We cannot stop the current.

We cannot rewind it.
We cannot force it forward.
We cannot jump ahead.

But we can surrender to it. We can trust the One who surrounds it all. And someday, when our journey through this current reaches its end, we will find ourselves standing on what Scripture calls new shores.

A new time.
A new realm.
A new understanding.

Revelation speaks of a new heaven and a new earth, and of a day when the sea is no more. We will step out of time and into eternity.

And there, in the presence of the One who held every moment, what we now see only in part will finally come into focus.

When Heaven Feels Closer

Imagine standing at the edge of a grand theater, heavy velvet curtains drawn closed.

The room is dim and quiet.

You can hear faint music. Muffled voices. The subtle movement of something happening just beyond the veil. You know there is life on the other side, but you cannot quite see it yet.

Then comes the whisper:

The curtain is thin.

That is what death is like for the believer.

Not an ending, but a veil.

Not silence, but transition.

Eternity is not far away.

It is closer than we realize, just beyond the curtain.

And the One who holds our lives in His hands is already there, preparing a place, setting the stage, ready to welcome us into the next act of His great story.

This is our wild hope beyond the veil. Faith does not stop at the miracle. It does not end with the answered prayer, the restored relationship, or the open door.

True wild faith keeps going.

It stretches into eternity.

It clings to hope when grief sits heavy.

It believes for heaven even when earth feels like it is falling apart.

It trusts not only in what God can do **here**, but in all He has prepared **there**.

To live with this kind of faith is to walk with eyes wide open, attentive to what is in front of us and anchored in what is ahead of us.

We live, love, and lead with heaven on our minds.

We stay ready, not in fear, but in anticipation.

We grieve differently, not without sorrow, but with the steady anchor of promise. We share the gospel not merely to ease consciences, but to awaken souls to the reality of eternity.

This kind of faith quiets fear.

It shakes off apathy.

It speaks peace into anxious questions about what lies beyond.

And it keeps our hearts burning with hope because we know how the story ends. Better still, we know the One who waits for us at the end of it.

So keep living.

Keep running.

Keep believing with eternity in view.

Because the finish line is not death.

It is glory.

And the torch you carry now does more than light your own path. It lights the way for others, all the way home.

Coaching Insight

The Big Truth

The wildest faith is not the faith that believes God only for what can be fixed in this life.

It is the faith that trusts Him with what cannot be finished here.

Living with eternity in mind changes how you suffer, how you love, and how you endure.

It anchors your hope beyond outcomes, beyond timelines, and even beyond death itself.

Wild faith does not deny the ache of living in a broken world.

It holds that ache alongside the promise that this world is not the end of the story. Eternity does not make faith impractical. It makes it unshakable.

The Mirror Question

Where have you been measuring faith only by what changes now?

What fears surface when you think about forever?

How might your life look different if eternity carried more weight than immediacy?

The Thirty First Footstep

Choose one area of your life where fear, grief, or urgency has narrowed your perspective.

Pause and intentionally reframe it through the lens of eternity.

Pray with heaven in mind. Speak hope out loud. Anchor your thoughts in what is promised rather than what is uncertain.

Faith deepens when you allow forever to shape how you live today.

The Inner Work

Thinking about eternity often surfaces anxiety rather than peace.

Fear of the unknown.
Fear of loss.
Fear of leaving unfinished things behind.

These fears are not signs of weak faith.

They are invitations to deeper trust.

Wild faith does not require you to fully understand eternity.

It invites you to trust the One who holds it.

When you release the need to control outcomes and timelines, you make room for a hope that outlasts fear.

Eternal faith grows when you stop asking how everything will end and start resting in who is waiting at the end.

Reflection Prompt

What emotions rise in you when you think about heaven or death? Where has fear of loss shaped how tightly you hold this life? What would it look like to live more fully now because eternity is secure?

Prayer of Alignment

Jesus, You have gone before me into eternity, and You hold every moment of my life in Your hands.

When my understanding feels small and my fear feels loud, anchor my heart in Your promise. Teach me to live with heaven on my mind and faith in my steps.

Help me grieve with hope, endure with courage, and love with urgency. I trust You with my life, my death, and everything in between.

Amen.

CHAPTER 12:
ROOTED IN THE WILD

Sustaining Faith When the Rush Fades

"Live so that when your children think of fairness caring and integrity they think of you."
— H Jackson Brown Jr.

The Shift from Movement to Maturity

There is a thrill in the early days of wild faith.

The adrenaline of obedience.
The fire of fresh vision.
The boldness that rises when God whispers, **Go.**

In those moments, trust feels electric. Prayer feels alive. Everything seems possible. But what happens after the miracle?

After the mission trip?
After the breakthrough?
After the mountaintop moment?

What do you do when the fire begins to dim, the answers take longer than expected, or the wild starts to feel more like wandering?

That is where many people lose heart. Not because they stop believing. But because they do not yet know how to stay rooted when the rush fades. Wild faith may begin with a roar.

But it is sustained by rhythm. Sustainability is not the opposite of wildness. It is the proof of it.

Anyone can run hard for a moment. But it takes a different kind of wild to keep showing up when the spotlight is gone and the feelings no longer follow.

Scripture is not only filled with people who leapt. It is filled with people who lasted. Noah built for years before the first drop of rain fell.

Anna prayed and waited in the temple for decades before she saw the Messiah. Paul wrote some of his most powerful words not from pulpits, but from prison.

This kind of enduring, rooted faith may not look loud. But it shakes heaven in ways that fire alone never could. Because in the end, it is not only about passion.

It is about presence. The presence of a person who still believes, still prays, and still loves, even when the rush is over.

If fire is what ignites us, rhythm is what sustains us.

Wild faith is not only a leap. It is a lifestyle.

And every lifestyle needs rhythm.

Jesus, the most Spirit-filled person to ever walk the earth, lived with rhythms of rest and renewal.

He withdrew often to quiet places. He rose early to pray. He honored Sabbath. He did not only pour out. He also paused.

And if Jesus needed those rhythms, how much more do we?

In a culture addicted to hustle, noise, and performance, we often confuse burnout with bravery.

But real courage is learning to stop before you collapse. Rhythms of prayer, rest, solitude, Scripture, and community are not soft disciplines for tame believers.

They are holy habits that keep wild faith alive. Because without rhythm, even the boldest fire eventually burns out. I remember coming out of Bible college full of fire.

My heart was blazing.
My vision felt clear.
I was ready to change the world one youth service at a time.

I stepped into my first youth pastor role with passion and expectation.

I had dreams of revival.
Of packed altars.
Of transformed teenagers.
Of a church set ablaze with the presence of God.

But I was not prepared for the undercurrents. Meetings that felt more like boardroom negotiations than ministry. Silent resistance to change.

Unspoken expectations. And what I would later come to recognize as church politics. It was disorienting.

I poured my heart out for nine months, trying to lead, trying to serve, trying to stay faithful. But the outcomes did not match the vision I had carried into that season.

Eventually, it all came to a quiet, painful end. And even though I met my wife during that season, a gift I will always treasure, I left that church carrying more than disappointment.

I left tired. I left disillusioned.

For almost a year, I wanted nothing to do with organized church. The flame had not gone out completely. But it was flickering.

And it was there, in that quiet in-between, that I had to discover something stronger than passion. I had to find rhythm. So many people begin with a burning yes to God.

Wide-eyed.
Sincere.
Ready to serve.

But eventually, almost every leader, dreamer, and disciple faces the same painful collision. The moment when zeal runs into disappointment.

When the people you thought would champion your calling remain silent. Or critical. When the systems you thought would support you feel more like walls than wings.

When the results do not match the prayers.

When the dream starts to feel heavier than holy.

These moments do not mean your faith has failed.

They mean your faith is being forged.

Disillusionment does not have to be the end.

It can become a threshold.

The place where faith shifts from hype to depth.

From reaction to formation.

From being fueled by applause to being anchored in obedience.

The question is not whether you will face these moments.

The question is:

What will you do when they come?

What rescued me from walking away wasn't a lightning-bolt moment or a breakthrough opportunity. It was rhythm.

The slow, sacred, almost hidden rhythm of returning to God when no one was watching.

Waking up early—not to perform, but to be still Opening the Word—not for a sermon, but for survival. Journaling raw prayers. Sitting in silence. Worshiping in my car when I didn't have the words.

Little by little, I found God again. Not in the roar of ministry, but in the rhythm beneath it. That's where wild faith is rebuilt.

Not on stages, but in secret places. Not in public victories, but in private surrender.

The rhythm beneath the roar is what keeps your soul alive when the noise fades. And it's what prepares you to roar again—this time with roots.

That season of rebuilding didn't just restore my faith. It reshaped my leadership. I stopped leading from pressure and started leading from presence. I learned that good sermons don't sustain you—God's voice does. That momentum is a gift, but maturity is a choice.

I began to see that leadership isn't about doing more, louder, or faster. It's about being rooted enough to lead others through their storms without losing your own anchor.

I became slower to speak and quicker to pray. More attentive to the quiet ones in the room. More intentional about rest, boundaries, and authenticity.

I started measuring impact differently. Not by numbers, but by transformation—first in me, then in others. Wild faith hadn't left me. It had gone deeper.

And from that place, I began to lead with a strength that didn't need a platform to be real. Friend, maybe you're there right now. Somewhere between the fire and the fatigue.

You started with passion. But life hit harder than you expected.

The results haven't come. The support didn't show up. The joy feels distant. And if you're honest, you've thought about quitting. Not just the role—but the calling. If that's you, you're not weak.

You're human. But what if this isn't the end? What if it's the beginning of something deeper? What if God is inviting you—not to run harder, but to root deeper? The wildness of your faith was never meant to be sustained by adrenaline.

It was meant to be sustained by rhythm.

Daily.
Quiet.
Deliberate rhythms that hold you steady when everything else shakes.

The question is not, *"Are you still on fire?"*

The better question is:

What rhythm is shaping your soul right now?

Sustaining wild faith is a lot like digging a well.

It's slow.
It's messy.
And most days, it feels like nothing is happening.

You strike rock.
You hit mud.
You wonder if you're wasting your time.

But those who keep digging eventually find water.

Not because they chased the rain but because they stayed long enough to reach something deeper. Surface-level faith runs dry in the heat of disappointment. But those who dig—through prayer, through stillness, through perseverance—find the underground stream that never stops flowing.

That's what rhythm is.

It's digging every day, even when the ground is hard.

It's choosing depth over drama.

It's building a life that holds water when the storms are gone and the crowds have moved on.

You don't need louder faith.

You need deeper roots.

And that starts by digging—again.

In John chapter 4, Jesus met a Samaritan woman at a literal well.

But what He offered her went far deeper.

"Whoever drinks the water I give them will never thirst.
Indeed, the water I give them will become in them a spring of water welling up to eternal life."

(John 4:14)

That's the kind of life we were made for. Not a surface-level faith that constantly needs refilling but an inner well, dug deep into the presence of God. That woman came looking for water in the heat of the day—worn out by shame and disappointment.

But she left with something eternal flowing inside of her. The same Jesus who met her at the well still meets us in our dry places today. He's not asking you to impress Him with your fire.

He's inviting you to let Him dig a well that will sustain you when the fire fades. Because the goal isn't just to burn brightly. It's to live deeply.

Staying Wild Without Burning Out

Wild faith was never meant to come at the cost of your soul.

I've walked through seasons where I was doing all the right things—leading, coaching, preaching, pouring out.

The calendar was full.
The opportunities were exciting.
The mission felt clear.

But underneath the momentum, I was exhausted. I had confused drive with faithfulness. And it was slowly burning me out. I didn't always recognize it right away. But I could feel it.

When joy felt distant.
When prayer felt heavy.
When my soul felt numb.

That's when God began to gently pull me back. Not through a breakdown but through an invitation.

He showed me something simple but life-changing: I didn't need a new assignment. I needed to return to rhythm.

I began to reclaim margin. Learning to leave space in my day for rest, reflection—even stillness. I reestablished boundaries. Not just with people, but with my own expectations.

I stopped measuring my worth by my productivity. I returned to the basics. I reconnected with God in ways that weren't tied to performance.

Soul care became non-negotiable. Sabbath became sacred again. Not a box to check but a weekly return to my identity as a son. Even my coaching began to shift.

I stopped showing up as someone who needed to have all the answers. And started showing up as someone willing to listen with God. And something unexpected happened. The fruit didn't disappear. It deepened. I had more to offer—not because I was doing more, but because I was more rooted.

If you're leading, building, parenting, or ministering with wild faith, hear this clearly:

You cannot sustain what you do not protect.

The fire of your calling needs the oxygen of rest. Passion without rhythm becomes pressure. But passion with rhythm becomes power. Staying wild doesn't mean staying busy. It means staying tethered.

To His pace.
To His peace.
To His presence.

That's where the strength is. That's where the fire is forged. Not in the frantic but in the faithful.

The Rhythm of Resting on Purpose

One of the most radical things you can do in a world obsessed with hustle is rest. Not just physical sleep. Soul rest. The kind of rest that says,

"I do not have to earn God's approval. I already have it."

Rest is not weakness. It is worship. It is trusting that God can do more with your surrender than you can with your striving. It is how Jesus lived. It is how creation began. Before Adam ever worked the ground, he rested with God.

That was his first full day. Rest is not what you do after you've proven yourself. It is where you begin to remember who you are.

In seasons of burnout and disappointment, I had to learn that Sabbath wasn't optional.

It was oxygen. A sacred rhythm that reminded me I am not a machine. I am a son. I am not the product of my productivity.

I am a beloved image-bearer, invited to walk—not sprint—with the One who made me. Rest doesn't put the fire out.

It protects it. Rest does not mean retreating from wild faith. It means rooting deeper into it. True rest is where strength is restored, vision is renewed, and identity is recentered.

It is in the quiet that God reminds us we are more than what we do. We are who He loves.

The world will always push you to keep producing, keep performing, and keep proving. But Jesus whispers something very different:

"Come to Me... and I will give you rest."

(Matthew 11:28)

Not just a nap.
Not just a break.
But a soul-deep exhale.

A place where you remember that He carries what you cannot. That is the rhythm of the rooted. They run when He says run.

And they rest when He says rest. They do not burn out because they are not burning alone. They burn with Him, not apart from Him.

And from that rested place, they rise again. Not frantic, but full. Not drained, but dangerous to the enemy. Because rested faith is resilient faith. And resilient faith is wild.

Sacred space with God rarely appears on its own. You have to make room for it. Sometimes that means blocking thirty minutes on your calendar just to sit quietly, journal, worship, or simply breathe with God.

Treat it like a meeting with the One who made you. Because that is exactly what it is.

These small spaces become anchors. They slow your soul enough to hear again. Another crucial rhythm is Sabbath.

Not as a legalistic duty, but as a gift. Choose one stretch of time each week to unplug from hustle, email, pressure, and performance. Let it become holy interruption. Use that time to do what restores your soul.

Take a walk.
Laugh with your family.
Eat slowly.
Pray without rushing.
Be still without needing to produce anything.

Sabbath reorients your life around one unshakable truth:

You are not the provider. God is.

Rest is not earned. It is received. Rest also requires a rhythm of release. Before bed, instead of scrolling, numbing, or carrying the whole day into the night, choose to quiet your soul.

Turn off the noise.

Read a Psalm.

Pray slowly.

Reflect on where you saw God that day. Let your body and spirit come down from the pace of performance. These small habits teach your heart how to release control and lean into peace.

And perhaps most importantly—let go of the guilt. Because rest can feel uncomfortable when your identity has been wrapped around what you do.

But remember this: Jesus rested. God Himself rested. You are not what you produce. You are who He loves.

When the voice of performance starts whispering again, answer it with truth.

Let God redefine success.

In His Kingdom, success is not speed.

It is not spotlight.

It is not constant output.

Success is obedience.

Success is presence.

Success is fruit that lasts.

So ask yourself, even in your busiest seasons:

Am I living from fullness, or am I trying to prove something?

Let that question shape your pace. Because the goal is not simply to rest. It is to live rooted—wild in faith and anchored in grace.

When God Feels Silent

There will come a time—maybe more than once—when God feels silent. When the prayers you once shouted feel like they hit a ceiling.

When worship feels hollow. When your quiet time feels more like wandering than encounter.

This is what many throughout history have called **the dark night of the soul—**

a season not of rebellion, but of refinement. It is not a failure of faith. It is often the very soil where faith grows up.

We do not like these seasons. They are disorienting—especially for those who are used to feeling close to God or being used powerfully.

But wild faith is not only about noise and momentum.

It is about depth.

It does not only roar on the mountain.

It also waits in the valley.

It listens when heaven seems still.

It weeps when the miracle does not come.

And it keeps walking when nothing feels certain.

These are the moments when we are tempted to believe something is wrong. But often, something deeper is being made right.

In the dark night, the roots go deeper. The applause fades. The momentum disappears. And all that remains is the quiet question rising from your own soul:

Will I still trust Him here?

If you are in that place, you are not alone. Elijah went there.

David lived there. And Jesus Himself cried out from the cross,

"My God, My God, why have You forsaken Me?"

Silence is not always abandonment. Sometimes it is the sacred hush before resurrection. So do not rush it. Do not numb it. Do not despise it.

This silence may be the very space where your faith stops performing and starts abiding.

Because the wildest faith is not always loud. Sometimes it is resilient. Sometimes it is rooted.

Sometimes it simply keeps walking—not because it feels God, but because it knows Him.

When God feels silent, the temptation is to pull back.

To stop praying.
To stop showing up.
To stop expecting.

But silence does not mean absence. It is often an invitation to shift your spiritual posture—from striving to abiding. In these seasons, you do not need a new strategy. You need a steady rhythm.

Small, faithful practices that keep you tethered—not to emotion, but to truth. Keep showing up.

Keep opening your Bible, even when the pages feel dry.

Keep talking to God, even when you are met with stillness.

Keep gathering with other believers, even when you feel out of sync.

Faith is not proven only in easy seasons. It is formed in empty ones. And your consistency in the silence becomes a declaration:

God is still at work, even when I cannot feel Him.

Anchor yourself in what you know. When your emotions become unreliable, go back to what is unchanging.

His promises still stand.

His character has not shifted.

He is still good.

He is still near.

Remind yourself of His faithfulness in your past and declare it over your present.

As David wrote:

"I remember the days of old; I meditate on all Your works; I consider the work of Your hands."

(Psalm 143:5)

Memory becomes a weapon when mystery surrounds you. And do not be afraid to lament. Silence is not a call to fake joy. It is an invitation into honest worship. Cry if you need to. Write prayers that sound more like ache than certainty. The Bible is full of wild prayers that sound more like protest than praise and God welcomes them.

You do not have to hide your pain.

You only have to bring it to Him.

Let other people hold faith with you.

Community matters deeply in silent seasons.

When your voice trembles, let someone else speak truth over you.

When your hands fall, let someone help lift them.

Sometimes the most spiritual thing you can do is send the text:

"I'm struggling. Can you pray for me?"

Wild faith does not always look like charging forward.

Sometimes it looks like letting someone walk beside you when you do not have the strength to move on your own.

These seasons will not last forever. But the roots you grow here will.

And one day, when the silence breaks and the light returns, you may look back and realize:

Your wild faith did not die in the dark.
It was deepened there.

Rooted for the Long Run

You were not made to burn out. You were made to bear fruit. Wild faith is not a sprint. It is a sacred endurance—

shaped in silence, formed in rhythm, and anchored in the presence of God. The goal is not to stay loud. The goal is to stay rooted. Whether you feel on fire, spiritually dry, or somewhere in between, the invitation is still the same:

Come back to the well.

Let God remind you who you are. Not a machine, but a son or daughter. Not a performer, but beloved. Faith that lasts does not come from doing more. It comes from digging deeper. So slow down. Breathe deeply. Let your faith take root. Because rooted faith is ready faith.

Ready for storms.
Ready for silence.
Ready for the next wild step—

even when you cannot yet see where it leads.

Coaching Insight

The Big Truth

Wild faith is not sustained by intensity. It is sustained by rootedness. When the rush fades and the feelings quiet, faith does not disappear. It is invited to deepen.

God is not asking you to stay loud. He is inviting you to stay connected. Faith that lasts is built through rhythm, presence, and daily return—not through constant momentum.

The Mirror Question

What has been shaping your soul more than the presence of God?

Where have you been relying on passion or pressure instead of rhythm and rest?

The Thirty First Footstep

Choose one simple rhythm that roots you rather than excites you. It may be a daily quiet moment, a weekly Sabbath practice, a short prayer before sleep, or a walk with God without an agenda.

Commit to returning to it consistently, not perfectly. Rooted faith grows through repetition, not intensity.

The Inner Work

When the rush fades, many people begin to fear that something is wrong. But often, that fear reveals a deeper belief:

That faith is only real when it feels productive, emotional, or visibly impactful.

Rooted faith invites you to release performance and rediscover identity.

You are not held together by how much you do. You are held by who you belong to.

As you learn to abide rather than strive, your faith becomes resilient instead of reactive.

And over time, what once felt ordinary becomes the very thing that keeps you anchored.

Reflection Prompt

What does your soul need more of right now—fire or faithfulness?

What rhythms help you feel anchored rather than driven?

Prayer of Alignment

God, teach me how to stay rooted when the noise fades and the pace slows.

I release the need to prove my faith through constant activity or visible results. Help me build rhythms that return me to Your presence again and again. When I feel dry, remind me that roots are still growing even when fruit is unseen.

Anchor my life in You, not in momentum, so that my faith endures for the long run.

Amen.

CHAPTER 13: STILL WILD

Living the Faith You Have Been Formed By

"Faith is not something to be understood. It is something to be lived"

— Søren Kierkegaard

If you have walked through these pages slowly, prayerfully, and honestly, I believe something has been stirred in you.

Not hype. Not pressure. Something quieter. Something deeper. A recognition that faith was never meant to stay contained inside ideas, moments, or chapters.

A remembering that wild faith does not end with agreement. It ends with embodiment. This final chapter is not here to give you something new.

It is here to help you carry what you already have. Wild faith is not a season you graduate from.

It is a way of living you return to again and again. It does not always roar. Sometimes it whispers. Sometimes it simply stays.

Still trusting. Still choosing. Still showing up when no one is watching.

I have learned this the hard way. There have been seasons when my faith felt loud and obvious and seasons when it felt quiet and almost invisible.

Times when obedience felt exhilarating and times when it felt costly and slow.

What I have discovered is this:

Faith does not disappear when it grows quieter. Often, it goes deeper.

You do not have to recreate the moments that first awakened your faith. You are not called to live on emotional highs or chase constant breakthroughs.

You are called to live awake. To live anchored.

To live responsive to God in the season you are standing in right now. That is the kind of faith that lasts. And that is the kind of faith that bears fruit.

This is **excellent**. It feels like the book is moving into its **closing wisdom**—and that's exactly what Chapter 13 should do.

You've shifted from:

- teaching the reader to
- **commissioning the reader**

That's powerful.

I refined this to:

- tighten cadence
- improve emotional clarity
- make the section feel more "book-final"
- preserve your voice and tone

The Faith You Carry Forward

If there is one truth I hope stays with you, it is this:

Wild faith is not about intensity. It is about alignment.

It is choosing trust when certainty is unavailable. It is choosing obedience when outcomes are unclear. It is choosing presence when productivity tempts you to measure your worth by results.

It is choosing love when fear would rather you withdraw. Wild faith looks different in every season.

Sometimes it runs. Sometimes it waits. Sometimes it wrestles. Sometimes it rests.

What makes it wild is not how dramatic it appears—but how deeply it remains surrendered. You will not always feel brave.

You will not always feel strong. You will not always feel close to God in the way you once did. None of that disqualifies you.

Faith is not sustained by feelings. It is sustained by faithfulness. And faithfulness often looks like small, repeated choices that no one applauds.

Showing up again. Praying again. Trusting again. Choosing love again.

This is how wild faith continues.

Living Forward Without Losing Yourself

There will be moments after this book when life feels loud again.

Responsibilities will press in.

Expectations will rise.

Disappointment may revisit you.

Do not assume something is wrong when that happens.

This is where the faith you have been forming gets tested—and strengthened.

When you feel tempted to rush, return to rhythm.

When you feel tempted to quit, return to presence.

When you feel tempted to perform, return to identity.

You do not need to prove your faith.

You are invited to live it.

Let your prayers stay honest.

Let your obedience stay simple.

Let your trust stay relational.

God is not asking you to manage the future.

He is asking you to walk with Him now.

Wild faith does not require constant motion.

It requires continual surrender.

A Life That Speaks

Whether you realize it or not, your life is teaching someone.

Someone is watching how you respond to pressure.

Someone is learning how to pray by listening to your words.

Someone is deciding what faith looks like by observing how you live it.

This is not meant to burden you.

It is meant to dignify the ordinary faithfulness of your life.

You do not need a platform to live with purpose.

You do not need perfection to lead with faith.

You do not need certainty to say yes.

You only need willingness.

Your wild faith will echo into places you may never see.

Into conversations you will never hear about.

Into courage that grows quietly in someone else because you chose to trust God in front of them.

Legacy is not something you leave behind later.

It is something you are living right now.

Still Wild

If the fire feels quieter than it once did, that does not mean it is gone.

It may mean it has gone deeper If your faith feels less dramatic than it once did, that does not mean it is weaker.

It may mean it is stronger than ever. If your obedience feels costly, unnoticed, or slow, you may be closer to the heart of God than you realize.

Wild faith is not always loud. It is not always visible. But it is always alive.

Still trusting.
Still choosing.
Still rooted.
Still wild.

And now, as you close this book, the story does not end. It continues in how you live.

In how you love.

In how you listen.

In how you take the next step God places in front of you.

May you run when it is time to run.

May you learn to rest when it is time to rest.

May you trust God in the in-between places.

May your faith remain honest, humble, and alive.

And may you never forget this:

Wild faith was never meant to be finished. It was meant to be lived.

Coaching Insight

The Big Truth

Wild faith is not something you finish. It is something you live. Formation always precedes fruit, and obedience always follows formation. This chapter is a reminder that the goal was never arrival, but alignment. God has been shaping you through risk, surrender, endurance, and trust so that your faith can be lived with integrity in ordinary days.

Still wild does not mean still intense.
It means still faithful.
Still available.
Still surrendered.

The Mirror Question

Where have you been tempted to measure your faith by feelings rather than faithfulness?

What rhythms or choices help you stay aligned with God when life feels ordinary or quiet?

What would it look like to live from formation rather than striving for impact?

The Thirty-First Footstep

Choose one practice that helps you stay grounded in God and commit to it as a rhythm rather than a reaction.

This might be:

- daily Scripture reading
- weekly Sabbath
- honest prayer
- journaling
- intentional rest

Do not choose what sounds impressive. Choose what is sustainable. Wild faith continues when alignment becomes habit.

The Inner Work

This chapter invites you to release the pressure to prove your faith and embrace the freedom to live it.

Many people confuse intensity with intimacy and movement with maturity. But faith deepens when identity becomes rooted and obedience becomes relational rather than performative. The inner work here is learning to trust that God is pleased with **presence, not production**.

Still wild faith grows when you allow yourself to live slowly, honestly, and consistently with God rather than chasing constant confirmation.

Reflection Prompt

What parts of your faith feel quieter now than they once did, and how might God be inviting you to see that as strength rather than loss?

Where do you sense peace replacing pressure, and how can you protect that shift?

Prayer of Alignment

God, thank You for the work You have done in me and the work You are still doing.

Help me live the faith You have formed in me without rushing ahead or shrinking back. Teach me to stay aligned when the path feels ordinary and faithful when the season feels quiet.

I release the need to prove myself and receive the invitation to walk with You daily. Keep my faith rooted, humble, and alive.

Amen.

A Wild Faith Covenant

Living What Has Been Awakened

This covenant is not a contract. It is not a vow of perfection. It is a holy intention to live what God has been forming within me.

I acknowledge that reading has shaped me, but living will define me. I recognize that faith is not something to admire from a distance, but something to embody in real life, in ordinary days, and in unseen moments.

I choose to carry forward what has been stirred in me, not through pressure, but through presence. I will not chase emotional highs or measure my faith by intensity. I will allow faith to mature through consistency, surrender, and trust.

I commit to returning to God again and again. When clarity is missing, I will choose trust. When fear rises, I will choose obedience. When disappointment visits, I will choose presence rather than withdrawal.

I accept that my faith will look different in different seasons. Sometimes it will run. Sometimes it will rest. Sometimes it will wrestle. Sometimes it will simply remain.

I release the need to prove my faith through performance, productivity, or comparison. I anchor my identity in who I am with God, not in what I accomplish for Him.

I commit to living awake to the sacredness of ordinary moments. I will listen for God's voice in daily rhythms. I will practice faithfulness even when outcomes are unseen. I will allow my life to speak louder than my words.

I acknowledge that others are watching how I live. Not to judge me, but to learn from my faithfulness. I choose to live in a way that invites others toward trust, courage, and hope.

I understand that wild faith does not always roar. It often whispers. It often stays. It often endures quietly.

I choose to remain still wild. Still trusting. Still surrendered. Still willing to walk with God one step at a time.

Today, I do not close this book as an ending. I receive it as a beginning.

Signed with intention and trust

Name: ______________________________________

Date: _________________________

EPILOGUE:
31 FEET FORWARD

The Charge to Keep Going

You've made it.

Page by page, story by story, you've stepped into the wild terrain of faith. You've felt the tug out of cages, the wind of calling, the burn of holy fire, the ache of surrender, the depth of discovery, and the glory of believing for more than this world can offer. Maybe your faith has been reignited. Maybe your eyes are open wider. Maybe your heart beats a little bolder now. I pray so.

But here's the truth:

This isn't the end of the book. It's the beginning of your charge.

Wild faith doesn't settle at the edge of understanding. It keeps going. Thirty-one feet forward. And then thirty-one more. And thirty-one more after that. It's not about having all the answers. It's about having enough faith to move toward the One who does.

You don't have to be fearless, just willing. You don't have to be qualified, just surrendered. You don't have to see the whole path, just the next step.

So, let me ask you:

What is your 31st foot?

That next place God is calling you to trust Him, love radically, forgive deeply, obey bravely, or dream again. Maybe it's a conversation you've been avoiding. A step of obedience that feels risky. A prayer that scares you to even say out loud. That's your 31st foot. That's where faith lives.

This book is not just words… it's a torch. And now, **it's in your hands**.

Take it. Run with it. Burn bright for those behind you. Walk rapture-ready, legacy-minded, and eternally focused.

Because wild faith isn't a chapter in your story, It's the headline. It's the soundtrack. It's the way of life for those who know this world is not their home.

Until the sky splits, until the trumpet sounds, until we see Him face to face,
Keep going.
Keep trusting.
Keep saying yes.

He's already waiting at the 31st foot.

AUTHOR'S NOTE:

The Story Behind 31 Feet Forward

I didn't write this book because I had it all figured out. I wrote it because I've lived it. I've wrestled with disappointment. I've questioned my calling. I've prayed bold prayers and walked through quiet seasons of surrender where nothing made sense. But through it all, God was writing something deeper in me, something wild and worthy. That "something" eventually became *31 Feet Forward.*

The name was born from a metaphor that wrecked me, inspired by the rhinoceros. Did you know a rhino can weigh over two tons and still run thirty miles per hour… all while only seeing thirty feet ahead? That's it. Beyond thirty feet? It's all unknown. But the rhino charges anyway. When I read that, something clicked in my spirit. **That's wild faith.**

Not waiting for the whole plan. Not needing all the answers. Just taking the next faithful step and trusting that God is already standing at foot 31. That one-foot mark beyond what I can see has become a symbol for my life, my ministry, and now my coaching practice. *31 Feet Forward Christian Coaching* was born out of this belief: that the life God has for us is found not in playing it safe, but in stepping out, even when the path is blurry.

For me, it's more than a coaching name. It's a calling. A legacy. A lifeline. It's the thread that ties together years of ministry, group home mission work, addiction recovery discipleship, church planting heartbreak, family resilience, and the messy joy of watching lives transform, one step of obedience at a time.

I don't know what your "31st foot" looks like. Maybe it's a conversation you're avoiding. Maybe it's a leap you've delayed. Maybe it's a prayer that feels too big to whisper out loud. Whatever it is, let me say this: **Don't wait for perfect conditions. Just move. Trust God. Step.** This world doesn't need more tame believers. It needs more runners. More torchbearers. More wild faith walkers who say yes to the unseen and light the way for others.

I'm cheering you on… 31 feet at a time.

With Wild Faith,
Joel

Appendix A:
How to Apply This Book to Your Life

Reading *Wild Faith* is only the beginning. Transformation comes not just through inspiration, but application. Below are practical steps to help you engage this book on a deeper level, so that its message doesn't just stay on the page but becomes part of your story.

1. Go One Chapter at a Time

Don't rush. Take one chapter per week. Let the stories, scriptures, and coaching tools settle into your spirit. Each chapter ends with **Reflection Questions**, **Journal Prompts**, **Action Steps**, and **Prayers**, use them.

- **Tip:** Create a weekly rhythm, one day to read, one day to journal, one day to act, and one day to reflect and pray.

2. Start a Wild Faith Journal

Keep a journal dedicated to your *Wild Faith* journey. After each chapter:

- Write your answers to the **journal prompt**
- Note down what God is saying through the **reflection questions**
- Record your prayers, struggles, and any "31st foot" moments

This becomes a spiritual record of your growth, your personal faith map.

3. Find a Faith Partner or Group

Wild faith is contagious. Share the journey with someone else.

- Invite a friend to read and discuss with you
- Start a *Wild Faith* group at your church or home
- Text or call each other weekly with updates on action steps or answered prayers

Accountability and shared courage multiply impact.

4. Practice the Coaching Tools

Each chapter ends with actionable tools designed to move your faith from concept to lifestyle. Don't just read them, **live them.**

- Take one action step per week
- Speak the affirmations aloud in the mirror
- Use the prayers as part of your daily rhythm
- Let the reflection questions guide your quiet time

These tools help shift your mindset, habits, and heart posture over time.

5. Create a 31 Feet Forward Plan

At the end of your reading journey, answer this question:

What is my 31st foot?

That next bold step of faith, however small or scary, is your launching point. Write it down. Pray about it. Share it with someone. Then…

Do it.

- Maybe it's a conversation you need to have
- A dream you've delayed
- A ministry you feel drawn to
- A healing journey you're ready to start
- A habit you need to build

God meets you in motion.

6. Revisit the Book in New Seasons

Wild faith evolves. You'll read these chapters differently in different seasons.

- When you're stuck, revisit **Chapter 1: No More Cages**
- When you're tired, go back to **Chapter 12: Rooted in the Wild**
- When you're dreaming, reread **Chapter 4: Born to Run**
- When life feels uncertain, meditate on **Chapter 11: The Wildest of Faith**

Let this book grow with you. Highlight it. Write in the margins. Make it yours.

7. Let God Write the Next Chapter

This book is not the end. It's a commissioning. You are now a **torchbearer**.

"You don't have to see the whole path. Just the next 31 feet."

So, walk forward. Burn bright. Believe big. And live your own *Wild Faith* story, one courageous step at a time.

APPENDIX B: PERSONAL COACHING TOOLS

Chapter 1 – Welcome to the Jungle

- **Reflection Question:** What "jungle" might God be inviting you into? A place of risk, surrender, and transformation?
- **Action Step:** Identify one area where you've been stuck in routine or fear.
- **Journal Prompt:** "God, I've grown used to the predictable. I've stayed where it feels safe. But deep down, I know you're calling me into the wild unknown with You. Help me name the place You're asking me to step into—and give me the courage to say yes."
- **Prayer:** Father, I confess I've often traded Your wild adventure for my own comfort. Forgive me for choosing safety over surrender. Today, I say yes. Lead me into the jungle, even if the path is overgrown. I trust You, not just with the outcome, but with the process. Help me hear Your voice above the noise, obey even when afraid, and walk closely with You in the wild. In Jesus' name, Amen.
- **Affirmation:** I was not made for the cage. I was made for the wild. I trust God one step at a time. Even in the jungle, He is with me. I will not shrink back; I will move forward in wild faith.

Chapter 2 – No More Cages

- **Reflection Question:** What fear has kept you in a cage?
- **Action Step:** Identify one cage and take one bold step outside it this week.
- **Journal Prompt:** Where have I seen fear hold me back from trusting God fully?
- **Prayer:** Lord, help me recognize the cages I've been living in and trust You enough to walk out in faith.
- **Affirmation:** I am no longer bound by fear. I walk in freedom and courage.

Chapter 3 – Born For The Wild

- **Reflection Question:** Where is God asking you to leave the familiar?
- **Action Step:** Take one uncomfortable step of obedience this week.
- **Journal Prompt:** Where has comfort been holding me back from full obedience?
- **Prayer:** Jesus, give me courage to leave the familiar and follow You wherever You lead.
- **Affirmation:** Comfort will not confine me. I choose obedience over ease.

Chapter 4 – Running Wild

- **Reflection Question:** What wild dream stirs your heart?
- **Action Step:** Share your wild dream with someone who will pray with you.
- **Journal Prompt:** What vision do I sense God birthing in me that feels wild and impossible?
- **Prayer:** God, breathe on the dream You've placed in me. Give me the boldness to run toward it.
- **Affirmation:** I was born to run in faith, not sit in fear.

Chapter 5 – Faith on Fire

- **Reflection Question:** What sparks your faith into action?
- **Action Step:** Engage in one intentional act that fans your faith flame.
- **Journal Prompt:** What fuels my faith? What drains it?
- **Prayer:** Holy Spirit, ignite fresh fire in my heart for what matters to You.
- **Affirmation:** My faith is not cold. I burn with purpose and passion.

Chapter 6 – Impossible Invitations

- **Reflection Question:** What invitation from God feels too big?

- **Action Step:** Write a prayer of surrender and say yes to the invitation.
- **Journal Prompt:** Where has God asked me to trust without knowing the outcome?
- **Prayer:** God, help me respond like Abraham—with faith that moves at Your word.
- **Affirmation:** I say yes to God's call. My impossible is His opportunity.

Chapter 7 – Prayers That Shake Heaven

- **Reflection Question:** What have you stopped praying boldly about?
- **Action Step:** Revive one bold prayer this week and pray it daily.
- **Journal Prompt:** What miracle have I stopped praying for?
- **Prayer:** Lord, stir in me a faith that prays like heaven listens—because it does.
- **Affirmation:** My prayers matter. I partner with heaven when I pray.

Chapter 8 – Into the Deep

- **Reflection Question:** Where is God inviting you into deeper trust?
- **Action Step:** Spend 10 minutes a day this week in stillness with God.
- **Journal Prompt:** Where in my faith journey do I feel like I'm just skimming the surface?
- **Prayer:** Jesus, take me deeper. I want to know You beyond the shallows.
- **Affirmation:** I am not afraid of the deep. I was made to dive into more of God.

Chapter 9 – On Mission Every Day

- **Reflection Question:** Where do your passion and purpose intersect?
- **Action Step:** Identify a mission field right in your daily life and serve.
- **Journal Prompt:** What mission field exists right in front of me?
- **Prayer:** Father, open my eyes to the mission opportunities around me. Use me today.
- **Affirmation:** I live on mission. My life speaks of God's love and power.

Chapter 10 – Passing the Torch

- **Reflection Question:** Who is watching your faith example?
- **Action Step:** Invest in someone younger through encouragement or prayer.
- **Journal Prompt:** What spiritual truths or life lessons do I feel called to pass on?
- **Prayer:** Lord, let my life burn bright for those watching behind me.
- **Affirmation:** I am a torchbearer. My faith is contagious. I live with legacy in mind.

Chapter 11 – The Wildest of Faith

- **Reflection Question:** How do you live with eternity in mind?
- **Action Step:** Start one conversation this week about heaven and hope.
- **Journal Prompt:** What fears or doubts do I carry about death or eternity?
- **Prayer:** Jesus, anchor me in eternity. Let my faith stretch beyond fear.
- **Affirmation:** I am anchored in eternity. I walk rapture-ready and full of hope.

Chapter 12 – Rooted in the Wild

- **Reflection Question:** Where do you need a rhythm of rest?
- **Action Step:** Block out one time this week for sabbath rest or renewal.
- **Journal Prompt:** Where in my life do I need to dig a deeper well of faith?
- **Prayer:** Father, root me in Your presence. Help me walk in sacred rhythm, not spiritual burnout.
- **Affirmation:** I am not what I produce. I am who God loves. I walk rooted, rested, and ready.

Chapter 13 – Still Wild

- **Reflection Question:** Where do you need a rhythm of rest?
- **Action Step:** Block out one time this week for sabbath rest or renewal.
- **Journal Prompt:** Where in my life do I need to dig a deeper well of faith?
- **Prayer:** Father, root me in Your presence. Help me walk in sacred rhythm, not spiritual burnout.
- **Affirmation:** I am not what I produce. I am who God loves. I walk rooted, rested, and ready.

APPENDIX C:
WILD FAITH GROUP DISCUSSION GUIDE

How to Use This Guide

This guide is designed to help groups move beyond conversation into transformation. It is not about having the right answers but about creating space where faith can be practiced, not just discussed.

Each session is designed for sixty to ninety minutes and follows a simple rhythm that can be repeated weekly. Leaders do not need to be experts. Your role is to guide the conversation, protect the space, and invite honesty.

Encourage participation but never force it. Silence is welcome. Vulnerability is honored. Growth happens at different speeds.

Suggested Weekly Session Flow

- Opening Prayer two to three minutes
- Check In or Icebreaker five to ten minutes
- Optional Video Clip or Reading Highlight five minutes
- Discussion Questions thirty to forty minutes
- Group Activity or Practice ten to fifteen minutes
- Closing Prayer and Blessing five minutes

Creating a Safe Group Environment

Before your first session, briefly establish these shared values.

- What is shared in the group stays in the group
- We listen to understand not to fix
- No one is required to share
- Silence is allowed and respected
- Every story matters

This creates trust and allows real faith work to happen.

Chapter 1 and Chapter 2

Welcome to the Jungle and No More Cages

Leader Note: These opening sessions are about awakening awareness. Help the group name where faith has become safe, routine, or constrained. Do not rush toward solutions. Naming the cage is the first act of courage.

Discussion Questions

- What cages of fear, habit, or expectation have you recognized in your life?
- How has comfort or predictability kept you from trusting God more fully?

Group Activity: Invite each person to name one cage they sense God is highlighting and one small step of obedience they will take this week.

Between Sessions: Pay attention to moments when fear or comfort tries to regain control. Notice without judgment.

Chapter 3

Born for the Wild

Leader Note: This session invites the group to confront comfortable Christianity. Expect some resistance. That is normal. Stay curious rather than confrontational.

Discussion Questions

- What does comfortable Christianity look like in your own life or culture
- How do you discern the difference between God's timing and fear of risk

Group Activity: Ask each participant to identify one area where comfort has replaced obedience and name one intentional disruption this week.

Between Sessions: Where did obedience feel costly this week and where did it bring freedom

Chapter 4

Running Wild

Leader Note: This chapter reconnects people with calling and holy desire. Create room for dreaming again without pressure to perform.

Discussion Questions

- What dreams or callings have stirred in your heart but felt too wild to pursue
- How does the rhino metaphor challenge or encourage your faith

Group Activity: Invite members to share past or present moments when they took a bold step of faith and what they learned from it.

Between Sessions: Pray daily for courage to take the next faithful step rather than the whole journey.

Chapter 5

Faith on Fire

Leader Note: This session explores ignition and refinement. Some may associate fire with pain. Hold space gently.

Discussion Questions:

- What tends to ignite your faith and what tends to drain it
- What catalytic moments has God used to reshape you

Group Activity: Have each person share one area where they want God to rekindle holy passion.

Between Sessions: Pay attention to what fuels your faith and what quietly extinguishes it.

Chapter 6

Impossible Invitations

Leader Note: This chapter requires courage. Normalize uncertainty. Obedience often begins before clarity.

Discussion Questions:

- What invitation from God has felt impossible or overwhelming
- What is currently stirring in your spirit that requires trust

Group Activity: Pray over each person's invitation and invite them to verbally say yes to God.

Between Sessions: Notice where fear shows up after saying yes and bring it honestly to God.

Chapter 7

Prayers That Shake Heaven

Leader Note: This session restores confidence in prayer. Expect spiritual hunger to surface.

Discussion Questions:

- How has prayer shaped your journey with God
- What does it look like to partner with heaven in prayer

Group Activity: Choose one bold prayer the group will agree on and pray daily for seven days.

Between Sessions: Record any shifts, answers, or resistance that arise while praying.

Chapter 8

Into the Deep

Leader Note: Depth requires stillness. Slow the pace of this session intentionally.

Discussion Questions:

- Where is God inviting you into deeper trust
- What keeps you in the shallow end spiritually

Group Activity: Spend a few minutes in quiet reflection before sharing. Silence is part of the work.

Between Sessions: Practice daily stillness even if it feels uncomfortable.

Chapter 9

On Mission Every Day

Leader Note: This session reframes mission as everyday faithfulness not performance.

Discussion Questions:

- Where are you already on mission and may not realize it
- What fears keep you from stepping into your assignment

Group Activity: Pair up and encourage one another daily for seven days in simple obedience.

Between Sessions: Watch for small opportunities to live on mission in ordinary moments.

Chapter 10

Passing the Torch

Leader Note: This chapter focuses on legacy. Keep the tone invitational not heavy.

Discussion Questions:

- Who passed the torch of faith to you
- Who might God be asking you to invest in

Group Activity: Invite each person to write a short prayer or blessing for someone younger in faith.

Between Sessions: Look for one opportunity to encourage the next generation intentionally.

Chapter 11

The Wildest of Faith

Leader Note: This session lifts the group's gaze toward eternity. Expect emotion.

Discussion Questions:

- What does it mean to live with eternity in mind
- How does heaven shape your daily choices

Group Activity: Invite the group to share one legacy they hope to leave.

Between Sessions: Live one day this week with eternity consciously in view.

Chapter 12

Rooted in the Wild

Leader Note: This session moves from intensity to sustainability.

Discussion Questions:

- Where are you trying to sustain wild faith with adrenaline instead of rhythm
- What rhythm needs restoring in your walk with God

Group Activity: Journal quietly then share one rhythm you will restore this week.

Between Sessions: Protect that rhythm even when life gets busy.

Chapter 13

Still Wild

Group Session and Commissioning

This final session is not about finishing a book. It is about beginning a way of life.

By this point in the journey, something has likely shifted. Faith has moved from concept to practice, from inspiration to formation. This session invites the group to name what has changed and to step forward with intention. Not louder faith. Not busier faith. Still wild faith.

As the leader, resist the urge to summarize everything. Let the group reflect, listen, and mark the moment. Transformation is often quieter than we expect.

Begin the session with prayer, inviting the Holy Spirit to help the group notice what has been formed and what is now being asked of them.

Group Conversation

Start by allowing space for reflection before discussion. Silence is welcome here.

Invite the group into conversation with these questions.

- What stood out to you most in this final chapter about living faith rather than just learning faith?
- Where do you sense God inviting you to embody wild faith in ordinary everyday life right now?
- In what ways has your faith matured or deepened since earlier seasons of intensity or passion?

As people share, listen for themes of surrender, steadiness, obedience, and trust. Affirm growth without comparison. Everyone's journey looks different.

Still Wild Reflection

Invite the group into ten minutes of quiet reflection or journaling with this prompt.

- Where am I being invited to live out wild faith more intentionally rather than waiting for a new moment or feeling?

After journaling, invite anyone who feels comfortable to share one simple way they want to live their faith more fully this week. Emphasize simplicity. This is not about grand gestures. It is about faithfulness.

The Thirty First Foot Commissioning

Transition the group by naming this truth out loud. Wild faith does not end with this book. It continues with the next faithful step.
Invite the group into a final conversation.

- What is your next thirty first foot of faith?
- How has your understanding of wild faith changed through this journey?

Encourage each person to name one concrete step they will take in the coming days. This could be a conversation, a boundary, a prayer practice, an act of obedience, or a decision they have been avoiding.

Group Commissioning Prayer

Gather the group in a circle if possible. Invite members to place a hand on the shoulder of the person next to them as a sign of shared journey and shared courage.

Pray a commissioning prayer such as this. God, thank You for the work You have done in us and among us. What You have formed here, we choose to carry forward. We do not ask for easier paths. We ask for faithful hearts. Give us courage to take the next step even when we cannot see beyond it. Teach us to live still wild, rooted in You, responsive to Your voice, and obedient in ordinary days. Send us out with trust, humility, and joy. Amen.

If desired, invite the group to speak a simple blessing over one another or to symbolically acknowledge the passing of the torch through prayer or spoken encouragement.

Leader Closing Encouragement

Remind the group of this truth.

You are not being sent out to perform faith. You are being sent out to live it.

Encourage the group to continue asking one question in the weeks ahead.

- What is my next faithful step?

The journey does not end here. It continues one obedient step at a time. Still trusting. Still choosing. Still wild.

A Note to the Small Group Leader

Thank you for saying yes.

You stepped into this role not because you had everything figured out, but because you were willing to walk with others honestly and faithfully. That willingness matters more than perfection ever could. Leading a group through *Wild Faith* was never about managing discussion or delivering insight. It was about creating space for God to meet people where they truly are, including you.

I want you to hear this clearly. Your presence mattered. Your consistency mattered. The way you listened, prayed, and stayed engaged even when conversations were messy or quiet mattered. God uses faithfulness in ordinary moments far more than polished leadership in impressive ones.

If at any point you felt inadequate, unsure, or stretched, you were exactly where a leader is meant to be. Wild faith is not formed in certainty. It is formed in obedience, humility, and trust. The same journey this group walked is the same journey God is still walking with you.

As you move forward, do not feel pressure to carry outcomes or measure success. Seeds were planted. Courage was stirred. Trust was practiced. That is holy work. God will tend what you helped nurture.

Thank you for leading with honesty, grace, and courage. Thank you for having wild faith.

With gratitude and deep respect,
Joel

REFERENCES

Assemblies of God USA. "Our History." *Assemblies of God*, Home | Assemblies of God (USA) .

Baker, Heidi, and Rolland Baker. *Always Enough: God's Miraculous Provision among the Poorest Children on Earth*. Chosen Books, 2003.

Batterson, Mark. *In a Pit with a Lion on a Snowy Day: How to Survive and Thrive When Opportunity Roars*. Multnomah Books, 2006.

The Bible. New International Version.

Bui, Winston. *When We Were Refugees*. Independent Publisher, 2020.

Eldredge, John. *Wild at Heart: Discovering the Secret of a Man's Soul*. Thomas Nelson, 2001.

Elliot, Jim. *Shadow of the Almighty: The Life and Testament of Jim Elliot*. Harper and Brothers, 1958.

Goff, Bob. *Dream Big: Know What You Want, Why You Want It, and What You're Going to Do About It*. Thomas Nelson, 2020.

Graham, Billy. *Facing Death and the Life After*. W Publishing Group, 1987.

The Hávamál. Translated by Lee M. Hollander, University of Texas Press, 1962.

Chariots of Fire. Directed by Hugh Hudson, Warner Bros., 1981.

Jarrett, Bryan. *Extravagant*. Charisma House, 2013.

Like Arrows. Directed by Alex Kendrick et al., FamilyLife Films, 2018.

Lewis, C. S. *Mere Christianity*. HarperOne, 2001.

Lucado, Max. *Anxious for Nothing: Finding Calm in a Chaotic World*. Thomas Nelson, 2017.

McManus, Erwin Raphael. *The Barbarian Way*. Thomas Nelson, 2005.

McManus, Erwin Raphael. *The Last Arrow*. WaterBrook, 2017.

Melville, Herman. *Moby Dick; or, The Whale*. Harper and Brothers, 1851.

Renner, Rick. *Sparkling Gems from the Greek*. Harrison House, 2003. www.renner.org.

Saint, Steve, and Mincaye. Personal testimony. Central Bible College chapel, Springfield, Missouri, early 2000s.

Schwarzenegger, Arnold. *Total Recall: My Unbelievably True Life Story*. Simon and Schuster, 2012.

The Smashing Pumpkins. "Bullet with Butterfly Wings." *Mellon Collie and the Infinite Sadness*, Virgin Records, 1995.

Synan, Vinson. *The Holiness Pentecostal Tradition: Charismatic Movements in the Twentieth Century*. Eerdmans, 1997.

Tenney, Tommy. *The God Chasers*. Destiny Image, 1998.

Tozer, A. W. *The Pursuit of God*. Christian Publications, 1948.

Van Gogh, Vincent. *Letters to Theo*. 1880s.

The Matrix. Directed by Lana and Lilly Wachowski, Warner Bros., 1999.

Washington, George. *Various Speeches and Writings*.

Wayne, Jimmy. *Walk to Beautiful*. Thomas Nelson, 2014.

Wigglesworth, Smith. *Ever Increasing Faith*. Gospel Publishing House, 1924.

Willard, Dallas. *The Divine Conspiracy: Rediscovering Our Hidden Life in God*. HarperOne, 1998.

Forrest Gump. Directed by Robert Zemeckis, Paramount Pictures, 1994.

Connect with the Author

Thank you for joining me on this wild faith journey. Whether this book stirred a bold next step, sparked fresh hope, or simply reminded you that you're not alone your part of a growing tribe of faith-filled believers saying yes to the unknown.

I'd love to stay connected.

Website: www.TeamWingo.com
Coaching Website: www.31feetforward.com
Instagram: @31feetforward
Facebook: facebook.com/31feetforward
Book Me to Speak or Coach: joel.wingo@31feetforward.com

If this book impacted you, I'd be honored if you'd leave a review or share it with someone else who's ready to live 31 feet forward in faith.

Together, let's keep charging forward, one step at a time.

With Wild Faith,
Joel Wingo

www.ingramcontent.com/pod-product-compliance
Lightning Source LLC
LaVergne TN
LVHW090513110826
845146LV00003B/844

* 9 7 9 8 9 9 5 5 0 4 6 0 3 *